The deck is stacked for
How to Cheat Your Friends at Poker

"Richard's so called wisdom, filtered through Penn's hilarious in-your-face writing style, fills the pages of *How to Cheat Your Friends at Poker*."
—*Los Angeles Times*

"A fast-talking handbook."
—*The Summerville Journal Scene*

"In addition to teaching you how to become the perfect weasel at card games—the false shuffle, how to shortchange the pot, and the kinds of jokes to tell while you're robbing your new friends blind—also provides step-by-step instructions on porking the host's wife."
—*Radar*

"Scabrous and without redeeming social value."
—*Publishers Weekly*

"Even if you never plan on cheating at the poker table, this book will help you defend yourself against those who do."
—*WOLV*

"This new book assures big winnings and no bad beats by teaching exactly what the title suggests."
—*ALL IN*

HOW TO CHEAT YOUR FRIENDS AT POKER

also by PENN JILLETTE

Sock

HOW TO CHEAT YOUR FRIENDS AT POKER

The **WISDOM** of **DICKIE RICHARD**

by PENN JILLETTE and **Mickey D. Lynn**

ST. MARTIN'S GRIFFIN ⚔ NEW YORK

LIBRARY OF CONGRESS CATALOGING-IN-PUBLICATION DATA

Jillette, Penn.
  How to cheat your friends at poker : the wisdom of Dickie Richard / Penn
Jillete and Mickey D. Lynn.
    p. cm.
  ISBN-13: 978-0-312-36068-9
  ISBN-10: 0-312-36068-1
  1. Cardsharping—Humor. 2. Poker—Humor. I. Lynn, Mickey D.
II. Title.

GV1247.J55 2005
795.412—dc22   2005046593

First St. Martin's Griffin Edition: October 2006

10 9 8 7 6 5 4 3 2 1

CONTENTS

DISCLAIMER

This book will teach you how to cheat. If you have any doubt about that, read the title again. It is *not* a book about how not to be cheated. The only way you can be sure you're not getting cheated is if you're doing all the cheating *and* all the winning. Anything short of that in poker and *you* are the fish. There are only two kinds of players in every game: the shark and the fish. If you aren't sure you're the shark who's there to win money, you're a fish who's there to lose money.

There really is no such thing as a *friendly game of poker*. People play games of chance in order to make money from the other people playing the game. There is no difference between fair play and cheating. Even "fair" poker is not a real job; it's a way to get something for nothing. And something for nothing—if it's winning the lottery or robbing a liquor store—is cheating. If you don't want to cheat, stop reading, sell this book on eBay for a couple bucks, and quit playing poker for the rest of your life.

If you want a fair game—don't play poker. If you don't want to cheat, someone else will. And even if no one is doing what *you* call cheating—if someone is just playing better—they're doing what *I* call cheating. Winning is all that matters, and if it's all that matters, then you'd better be winning any way you can. By any means necessary. . . . I'll lay you seven to five that Malcolm Little played a bit of poker.

If you're looking for honest money, get a job. If you're looking for fun, buy a hooker. If you're looking to hang out, go to a gay bar. If you're looking to make some money in home poker games . . . keep reading.

INTRODUCTION
by Penn Jillette

I don't feel good about this book.

I am not a card cheat. I have never been a card cheat. I don't think anyone should be a card cheat. I don't think *you* should be a card cheat. I sure don't want to help you be a card cheat.

Doing magic is not cheating. Writing shows and books is not lying. At some level everything I write is fiction, and everyone is supposed to be in on it. When I pick up a deck of cards to do a trick, everyone knows it's not on the up-and-up—it's a trick and everyone knows it. On the rare occasions when I play a real game of cards, I don't cheat. When I play with friends, we don't play for money, and there's no cheating. Why bother?

When I play cards on *Celebrity Poker Showdown* or in little Texas Hold 'Em tournaments in Vegas, I promise everyone I won't cheat. I give my word. It's not like I really have to. I don't win, so no one would care if I *were* cheating. As this book will show, you *can* cheat in Vegas, but why bother? To make money cheating in Vegas takes a lot of work. To make money cheating at home games is much easier. It's bringing a gun to a knife fight, and you're fighting against people who like you and don't want to hurt you. Candy from babies.

Cheating at home card games is stealing from friends. It's as easy as that. The techniques are easy. The work is easy. All that makes it hard is the morals, and unfortunately there are ways to get over that problem. Sadly, this book will help.

Where does your loyalty lie, with people or ideas? Would you perjure yourself for someone you loved? Would you turn in your Unabomber brother? Would you act as a front for a book that you're not sure should be published? I guess you're not the one to ask, since you're reading a book about how to cheat your friends. Your loyalty is to neither people nor ideals.

Many years ago, when I was a kid hitchhiking around the country, I met a guy. For this book, we're going to call him *Dickie Richard*. (It's not his real name. He let me choose the fake name, so fuck him.)

I was eighteen years old. I was a good juggler, a good talker, and I did a little magic. I was hoping to be the great existential American writer, but I was afraid that I might have to get a job. All my options were still open. I did a lot of card tricks. When I met Dickie I briefly considered becoming a card cheat. To a kid, it's very sexy. Magic isn't sexy; cheating is. Dickie is as colorful as you can get. He drips character. He's a totally fictitious character, talking large and cutting up jackpots (that's slang for "telling stories"). I figured if I couldn't make it as a writer, and if I couldn't make it as a performer . . . well, being Dickie might be a good third option. Dad always told me I should have something to fall back on. Dad didn't mean cheating.

Dickie watched me juggle and he watched me with a deck of cards. He listened to me talk and make jokes. He saw how I handled myself. He taught me some amazing card moves. He bought me food and he gave me a place to stay. He told me stories. He taught me a lot about cheating at cards. He taught me a lot about cheating at life. The cards don't matter. Once you decide to cheat, it doesn't matter much what you're cheating at.

It's pretty easy to see why a kid who played with cards would want to hang out with a real, full-time card cheat. It's harder to see why Dickie would want to hang out with me. It was only a couple of months, but that's a lot of time to waste on a kid. I was a big guy, and I was living on the streets, trying to look tough and maybe succeeding a little. Dickie had some money he needed to pick up, and maybe he wanted someone like me standing beside him. I didn't understand what errand we were running at the time, and I don't understand it much better now.

Dickie isn't just a card cheat—he does other bad stuff, too. And even if he did use me for backup, a little fake muscle wasn't worth the time he spent with me and the information he gave me. He wasn't trying to screw me in any sense of that word. I wasn't his type to screw and I had nothing to be screwed out of. For some reason, he took a liking to me. I seemed sleazy enough to be an apprentice, but I don't think he wanted an apprentice. Dickie opened up to me and taught me a lot. At the time, it was amazing—I never thought people like him even *existed,* much less that I would get to know them. Now that I'm older, and I know more about Dickie and more about the world, it's even more amazing. He didn't know me. He lies to everyone. Why would he tell *me* the truth? He lives a secret life. Why would he talk to me? I was a kid living on the streets, hitching across the country. What was in it for him?

I hitchhiked all over the USA. It was always a mystery why anyone gave me a ride. It's so much easier and safer not to stop. Other hitchers told me about men or women that gave rides because they wanted sex, but, sadly, I never had that happen. Some people picked me up to pay off some sort of cosmic debt, to pay back a favor a stranger did for them. For some it was political—Power to the people. Right on. Some people picked me up so they could talk to someone who didn't know any of the people they knew. They picked me up *because* I was a stranger. They could spill their guts to someone who could never use it against them. Never. I rode across America listening to stories of bad marriages and bad bosses. I heard about dreams of heavy metal superstardom from a balding trucker whose friends wouldn't know anyone beyond Skynyrd. Picking up a hitch-hiker for a talk session is cheaper than paying a therapist. Maybe that was Dickie's motive: He wanted to spill the beans to someone, and I was a handy choice. I couldn't blow his cover. I would never meet any of his marks. With my hair and my clothes and my age, I couldn't get into any of his country clubs. I would never meet his "friends." I couldn't hurt him. Dickie's not the kind of guy that needs to talk, but maybe everyone likes to talk a little. Cheating at cards is a very lonely life; if you make a friend, you rip them off. I remember a story about Abbie Hoffman, after his surgery and his new identity and years on the lam, looking in a mirror and scream-ing "Abbie Hoffman" at his reflection. Maybe that's what this book is all about: Dickie just needed to scream.

I think my mom and dad made it so that I could never really be a cheat, but Dickie helped me decide that I didn't *want* to be a cheat. He loves what he is, but he told me to aim higher. He gave me advice and not a small amount of money to keep me going and get me started. He dropped me off on the highway, and I headed back to the East Coast. I had enough of Dickie's ill-gotten jingle in my pocket to get off the road and get a place to stay, and enough of his hard-earned ideas in my head to get me started on the road to my very good life. When he left me off at the entrance ramp, I said, "I owe you, man." It was honest. It was romantic.

Over the years, when the Penn & Teller tour would come to whatever area he would happen to be in, Dickie would surprise me. He would come to the show and hang with me backstage after. Once or twice, I took him out to dinner with a bunch of my friends. I was

Mr. Bigshot. I'd take us all to nice restaurants and tell some of the safe stories about Dickie and me. I'd always say, "I owe Dickie big-time" or something equally showbizzy shallow.

He'd sometimes get in touch when he was going to be in L.A., to see if I had any rich Hollywood friends that I could get him in a game with. I was lucky—I don't have rich friends that gamble, so I didn't have to lie. Then, a couple of years ago, Dickie really called my bluff. I hadn't seen him in years. I got an e-mail from a friend about another friend of a friend having met a guy who wanted my e-mail address for a guy named *Dickie Richard*. I was thrilled. Dickie was in the twenty-first century. I dropped him an e-mail. We started writing back and forth. "Do you really owe me, cowboy, or was that bullshit?"

Like an idiot, I wrote back, "I really owe you, brother."

So he asked me for a favor. He wanted me to "put out his book." I'm not a publisher, but Dickie didn't care. He wanted me to "put out his book." Dickie has made plenty of money as a cheat. He doesn't even cheat much anymore. Well, he doesn't actively seek out people to cheat. He's retired, but when there's opportunity he always takes it. Seize the sucker. To pass his time in semi-retirement, he wrote a book. He wanted me to help him get the book published.

No problem; I did owe him. I told him I'd pass his book along to people who could publish it. It seemed there might be a market. Poker is big now, and there are lots of home games to cheat at. Hey, it wouldn't be on my head. But he wasn't happy with me just passing his book along. "You owe me; I want you to make sure my book comes out." I couldn't guarantee that. He sent me his "book." It was a collection of random rambling stories, tips, philosophy, and lots of bragging. It was shit. He said he wanted it to come out under my name. He said that I'd made money selling books and I had "a name," and he wanted me to put my name on it, change it to my style, and give him all the money.

Jesus Christ.

Here's one thing you can learn from this introduction: Don't take money from a cheat. Just don't.

I told him no one would believe I'd written it. I'm showbiz—I'm not the real deal. I'm a phony. Some people saw me play cards on TV. I suck. I've been working in theater ever since Dickie dropped me off on the highway. I didn't have time to learn all this stuff. It's not my book. I told Dickie I'd find someone to front for his book—I have a magician friend that could do all the moves and could do interviews about the book. Dickie said no, I owed him, and he wanted *me* to put out his book.

I told Dickie that I'd write an intro and pimp it to the publishers that I've worked with. I told him that I'd use a false name for him and never give up who he was. I told him I'd clean it up and punch it up. He wanted cash. I told him if I could sell his piece-of-shit book, I'd take the checks made out to me and give him the money in cash. Dickie loves cash. He really loves cash. He didn't want any checks going from me to him. I don't know what he's thinking. The fact is, he tells stories in this book that his fish will recognize, and they give him away. If anyone he's ever cheated reads this book, they'll know who Dickie is, and they'll know they were cheated. He rarely used false names, and they'll remember his name. They'll try to find him, and I don't think it'll be that hard. But he didn't care about that; he just didn't want a "paper trail" from me. I guess I get to pay the income tax, too. The income tax may be the whole thing. What an asshole.

I've been working on this book for a year. I got my friend Mickey Lynn—a writer, poker player, and amateur magician—to help me with it. Mickey worked his ass off. We've tried to edit it and organize it, and we even threw in a joke or two. We didn't just fix grammar and spelling—we wrote most of the goddamn book.

I guess my allegiance is to people, not ideas. This book proves that. I did a lot of work to teach you how to cheat your friends. I hope you enjoy the book and learn from it. And I hope that what you learn is that you don't want to cheat and that you want to avoid situations where you can be cheated. I hope that's what you learn. If you do decide to be like Dickie, try to make the world more interesting while you steal from people who trust you. At least Dickie did that. I think that Dickie being Dickie was worth at least some of what he ripped off.

Mostly, I hope that if this book turns you into a card cheat, and you happen to give some juggler/magician/comedian a start in showbiz . . . I hope the kid you help has the common sense to never say "I owe you."

He found a way to fuck me.

∘ Chapter 1 ∘

YOU'RE NOT PLAYING A GAME

D o you want to cheat because you love playing poker? Throw away this book—you've just been ripped off. You wasted your money. The people who love to play poker are the people who are going to be giving you money. You care about money, not poker. This is not a book on learning to play poker, or about loving to play poker: This is a book about making money. Wasn't the title clear enough for you? You're reading this book to learn how to cheat people out of their money in friendly home games of poker. Get it?

To cheat at home poker games, you do need to know *how* to play poker. Get a couple of books and learn the game. Learn the rules you're going to be breaking, and learn a little of the strategy you're not going to be using. You need to know what your losers will be thinking.

Get any one of the little BS books that'll tell you the rules and how to play. Learn all the stupid games. Learn Blind Man's Bluff where you stick cards to your head. Learn Crazy Pineapple with one-eyed jacks and deuces wild. Any book will do. You don't care very much about any of the strategies—your strategy will be cheating. If you're happy with the amount of money you can win playing honestly, this book isn't for you. Throw the book away.

No Limit Texas Hold 'Em is the big game these days. It's what they play on TV, and every jerk off who watches the *World Series of Poker* wants to play Hold 'Em. They want to play it in the casinos and they want to play it at home. Most of the stories in this book will be about Hold 'Em because most people know that game. Ten years ago, it was seven stud and before that it was five-card draw. Hold 'Em is a fine game, and its popularity will only help you make money. But there are a lot of games out there, and you need to know all of them. The focus here is mostly on No Limit Hold 'Em so you won't get confused. You can (and will) cheat at every game you find.

If you're telling yourself that you're just reading this book to learn how not to be cheated by someone else, don't bother. The best way to not be cheated is to not play for money. If you play cards for money, you're going to be cheated, and you deserve to be cheated. People who play fair get money by working. If you're trying to get money without working, you're cheating, and if you're cheating, someone else is going to be better at it. I'm going to be better at it. If you let me, I'll make you better at it.

If you follow this book—if you take what I've learned from a life of full-time cheating, and you *really* learn it and do it *just* the way I explain—you can make money, and plenty of it, without working. If you're going to take this book seriously, promise yourself right now that you will never work again. Never! You cheat or you work. There is no in-between. Those are the two ways of life. Biff down at my dry cleaning store—he works. He works like a Chinaman. Bill Gates? He doesn't work. I don't work. You don't have to work.

You're not going to be playing cards and you're not going to be working at playing cards. You're going to be cheating. I know a thing or two about cheating. You can trust me—I do nothing but cheat. I have large bank accounts in many cities and towns across the country. I own four houses and a mobile home. I have seven cars and two of them are really nice. I have over five grand in my pocket right now as you read this. I would say that I never have to work again . . . except I never worked before. I never have to work, and you don't have to work, either. If you want to cheat, I can show you how.

Step one: Learn how to play all of the games and get used to the fact that you're never going to play any of the games again. You'll sit at the table, you'll hold cards, you'll make bets—but you won't be playing. You'll be cheating. You'll be cheating your keister off and no one will know it. And if they do know it, who cares? There will be other towns and other suckers.

Chapter 2

HI-HO, HI-HO, IT'S OFF TO WORK I GO

H ere's a typical workday.

Tuesday, I get up at 2 P.M. and have some "breakfast." I read the paper and have a few cups of coffee. My lunch is a nice meal out. I leave for work at about 7:30 P.M. I pull into the driveway of a very nice home. The driveway is really its own street and I check out the cars that are parked there. These are owned by my "friends." There are a couple of BMWs, a Lincoln, and one of those really fancy Porsche jobs that tells me more than I need to know about the private parts of the owner. I walk up the long brick path to the massive oak doors and ring the bell.

My host's second wife, Tina, answers the door. Nice. I smile and give her a wink—we'd met briefly at the driving range where I'd met her husband just a week before. The wink is the only real gamble I'll take all night and it will pay off. I pull out a bottle of wine (tied with a bow) from behind my back and give it to her. She smiles, squeezes my arm, and leads me into their family room. The pool table has been pushed aside to make room for a very nice poker spread.

"Hey, Todd, how are the kids?" I ask.

"Hey hey! I'm so glad you made it by." Todd stands up, an expensive stogie in his teeth. He has a stupid green banker's visor pulled low on his forehead. He's ready for fun. "The kids are great, off skiing right now."

Todd introduces me to the rest of the players at the table: two lawyers, a dentist, and a couple of local businessmen. "And hey, Dickie, what racket did you say you're in?"

"Human resources," I reply. Dull. Non-threatening. Perfect. These guys won't be asking about my work.

I buy in, sit down, and they deal me in. One of the lawyers has a three-thousand-dollar watch and a tie that cost more than my first car. He throws his chips around freely like money means nothing to him, but he sure doesn't like to lose. I can tell. You know how I can tell? No one likes to lose.

The dentist comes over the top of me in an early pot; he plays tight, but aggressive. He reads all the poker books and follows the advice to the letter. He knows he's not a chump.

"If you don't win this pot, you're going to have to sell off your extra gold fillings," I joke. Everyone laughs. That's a good joke for this table. Not funny. Not witty. Not clever. Comfortable. Real funniness puts people on edge. This is a friendly game. We're just guys.

Todd, who has family money, plays badly. He starts out on tilt. Good, I could let someone else get his money. I let the movement of chips on the table happen fairly naturally. Todd loses a bundle and builds up the pot for lawyer number one. There are only three players with significant stacks of chips: the lawyer, the dentist, and . . . me. You know the name of this book, so that shouldn't be a shock. It is a little surprising (I don't like big surprises) to the rest of the table because they never see me win anything big. I steal a few small pots once in a while, but I just fade into the background, making pleasant conversation, keeping it friendly. We're just hanging around playing some cards. I haven't done much of anything yet.

My host deals. I cut the cards and talk about an interesting lawsuit I'd read about in the paper. The lawyer perks up a bit. "My firm's handling that," he says. "We're going to try suing the teacher's union for breach of contract."

The dentist clacks his tongue and rolls his eyes. "It's wrong, you know. They're underpaid already, and you guys are going to bleed them dry from both ends."

"Hey," snaps the lawyer, "you had no problems with what I do when you needed me to settle that little root canal problem. If you don't approve of lawyers, make sure you always get the right tooth, okay?" Beautiful.

There's an awkward pause in the conversation as Todd deals the cards. "It's a good thing you're not a proctologist," I say, and the table chuckles. I get my cards and watch as the lawyer—let's call him Hammy—peeks at his cards. Hammy's eyes get wide and he shoots looks at everyone's chips at the table. With tells like that, you hardly need to cheat. He makes a big bet, and the dentist—Rummy—immediately raises. I shrug and call. What the hell . . .

Hammy re-raises. Rummy calls, and after a lot of thought, I call, too. Wow, somebody has good cards. If only there were some way to know what cards the other people have, poker would be so much easier. And more profitable.

The flop comes and there's another flurry of betting. Hammy makes a big bet, big raise by Rummy, I call. A re-raise, a re-re-raise, someone's all-in. They're both all-in. I reluctantly go along for the ride. There's more than nine grand on the table with two cards to go. This hand has me up against the big winners of the evening, so almost all the chips are on the table.

We show our hands. The lawyer and the dentist each have an ace in their hands, and another two aces come out on the flop. I've got pocket jacks. The turn helps no one, and Rummy is a huge favorite with his king kicker. There are only two cards in the deck that will let me win the pot. The odds are twenty to one against me. Or maybe they're 100 percent in my favor.

Gee, miracles happen and I get a jack. Rummy laughs and makes a move to rake in the pot. He doesn't notice right away that, even though my three jacks don't beat his three aces, I have a full boat—jacks over aces. I take down the pot, and Rummy and Hammy are both shocked. I'm, delighted yet gracious—I know how it feels to lose and I don't want to rub their faces in it. I want to be friends with these guys for at least a few more weeks.

The money they lost was a few hours' work for each of them. It's less than they save by cheating on their taxes each year—by a lot. It was the most action they've ever had in their little game. They each lost a few thousand dollars, and yet . . . they're happy for me. They're a little testy with each other, but they'll come back the next week. So will I.

I dump a hundred bucks to Todd a couple of hands later (I want him to remember that poker can be fun), and then I call it a night. I make sure I shake everyone's hand—even Tightwad, the businessman who only played four hands all night. "It's better to be lucky than good," I say to the crowd, as Tina escorts me to the door.

"I bet you're good, too," she says quietly as she hands me my coat. I give her a wink and head out into the night.

Gross:	
Winnings	$9,350.00
Expenses:	
$ .36 per mile	$21.60
Bottle of wine with bow	$43.84
Round of golf for my foursome at the country club	$540.00
Caddie tips	$80.00
"Another round" of drinks with tip	$30.00
Profit	$8,600.00

I left my place at 7:30 P.M. and was knocking back at the bar near my hotel by 1:15 A.M. I spent some time and money setting up this game. The week before, I was at the country club for five hours, but I got leads on another two games, and this wouldn't be my last game at Todd's place. So let's figure an hour for setting up this game and six hours of play. That's $1,225 an hour.

Over a grand an hour. That's not counting practice, but I don't practice much anymore. I keep my moves clean in the mirror, but I don't have to do that too often because I'm always using them. Over a grand an hour for a kid who didn't finish high school.

Tuesday was a pretty good haul. I don't do that every game, but I keep my hourly above $750 or I move on to another game.

Yeah, it's a good living, but it's not steady, right? I play between one and six games a week. I move around a lot, so I'm only really making money about thirty weeks a year. A couple of years I broke a half million. I haven't dipped below six figures a year in the last decade.

It's nice work. And you can get it.

Chapter 3
SLANG

I use a lot of phraseology in this book that I've picked up by spending most of my life playing and cheating at cards. There are definitions in the back if you can't figure out what something means.

You don't want to start using gambler's slang. Why would you? If you're going to a game, would you wear a T-shirt that says CHEATER across the chest?

I put the slang in the book because it might be useful for you to know it. I also know that there are a lot of fools who think that if they use the lingo, they'll be showing the world that they're an "insider." All they'll be showing is that they read a book. You don't want to make that mistake.

Use slang when other people use slang. If people say "Czechoslovakia" instead of "check," you can do it, too, if you want. If your friends talk about the Holy City or having fishhooks, feel free to join in. A lot of players love that bullshit, and you want them to have fun. Poker is a game that has a lot of cutesy expressions and traditions, and home games are where people get to live out their fantasies of being a professional gambler, or a cowboy, or a tough guy.

If someone asks you if you've got *work* down, you should know what they're talking about, but never let on that you know what they're talking about. If they ask you where you learned to deal *from the basement*, you should ask them what they mean and play dumb. Never use insider jargon when talking about cheating. Never. In fact, never talk about cheating—period.

Players pick up slang, and then they like to throw it out there to show that they're savvy. Don't take the bait. Usually, they're just showing off. They want people at the table to think they know the game. Let them enjoy their loser fantasies.

Once in a blue moon, you'll bump up against another cheater. He might use slang to try and find out if you want to partner up, or he might use it to get information from you. Don't do it. Play dumb, and never let on that you know any of the information in this book. If you start gabbing about *pegging* or *seconds* or *copping from the pot*, you're admitting you know about cheating. If people think you know about it, they'll think you can do it, and you don't want them thinking that way.

Don't show off. Don't pretend that reading this book makes you some kind of genius. It doesn't. It makes you someone who can buy a book. You should know the slang, and the book will sell more copies if it's in here. But if you memorize it and then use it during games to try and intimidate people, you should learn another term: jackass.

○ Chapter 4 ○

FINDING THE LINE (OR, GOOD MONEY FROM BAD PEOPLE)

You want to cheat at cards and still sleep better at night? You want to believe there are times when cheating is okay? You want to take the moral high ground? You're jerking yourself off.

If you're married and you call your wife to tell her how busy you are on your business trip, and you're really holed up at the local fleabag motel in the same town banging your secretary . . . that's wrong.

If you call your wife late (because you lost track of time) when you're hanging out with your friends, (when she's expecting you home for dinner) and you tell her that you had a lot of extra work at the office . . . is that wrong?

You steal a BMW, you're evil. You steal a loaf of bread to feed your family, you're the hero in some political novel . . . right? Wrong. It's all wrong. You can fool some of the people some of the time and all the people once in a great while, but you can fool yourself every fucking second.

Anyone who tries to pretend that these moral situations are different from one another is just making excuses. Lying is either wrong or it isn't. Stealing is either wrong or it isn't. Save your justifications for Saint Peter; maybe he'll buy your shit.

"It doesn't hurt anyone" is a great excuse. Is something unethical or immoral only if someone gets hurt? If you steal ten grand from a lawyer, he's not hurt. Hell, he'll probably find a way to write it off. If you win a hundred bucks from a factory worker fair and square, is that okay? He may not be able to afford to lose that money, so maybe his kids won't get potato chips and cookies with lunch that week. You hurt him without cheating. His kids have been hurt, too (the fat little bastards).

"He went into the game willingly. We all understood the rules. I could have lost, and I would have accepted that."

You think people really understand the rules? Everybody understands that if you gamble in Vegas, the house wins. Those billion-dollar hotels aren't built with happy thoughts. When some guy bets his puny life savings on red on the roulette wheel and it comes up black, does he go to the casino manager and say, "I didn't think I'd lose, I didn't understand?" He doesn't get a second try. He's fucked. And he should know better. People say they understand that the house wins, but they don't really, they think they're the exception.

Everyone wants a free ride on the morality train. If you tell your wife that you want to fuck around on the side, and then fuck around, is that okay? Is that better than just doing it? Is it better than doing it when she never finds out? Is telling your secretary that you might give him (I'm not sexist) a raise at the end of the year better than telling him that there's no way you're going to give him more money? What if you believe you might give him a raise if, for instance, you happen to win the Lotto? (What has five balls and fucks Mexicans? Lotto.)

Golly, gosh, gee whiz, these are hard questions. No, they're not. The answer is simple and the answer to all of them is the same: Morality is what you make of it. If you're okay with it, it's moral.

End of story. If you feel bad because of your own decisions, then you shouldn't have made those decisions. If you aren't comfortable taking people's money with a deck of cards, maybe you picked the wrong fucking book. Maybe you meant to grab *Chicken Soup for the Card Cheat's Soul.* You live with yourself, you make amends, or you kill yourself. I don't really care—you're not going to leave me your money. You know where your own line is. And if you don't know where your own line is, how are you ever going to make a good guess about where someone else's is?

If you need a list of reasons why cheating is okay, you shouldn't cheat. Just get a job. Don't play cards for money. You know whether it's right or wrong. There is no gray area. If you're winning at cards, you're taking someone's money unfairly. Playing cards is not an honest job. Go cure fucking cancer. Pretending that "advantage play" is in any way different from swiping an old lady's purse is just a waste of time. Accept what you're doing or don't do it. It's that easy. Don't do it and then expect to forgive yourself. You've done enough lying to yourself. You bought this book because it had a funny cover, right?

Cheating a cheater is the same as cheating a straight player. That's why they call it cheating. You're not fucking Robin Hood (that's Maid Marian's job). You're not a vigilante. If someone else is breaking the rules, does that make your cheating okay? No. What makes cheating okay is being okay with cheating. If someone punches me, then they did something bad, whether I deserved it or not—and I probably did. If I hit him back, would you think two wrongs make a right? What if some law enforcement professional hits me? Society gave him the authority to hit me, so it's beyond right and wrong? Bullshit—he's a pig.

Is cheating at cards wrong if you take all the money and give it to a worthwhile charity? The players were prepared to lose the money anyway, or they wouldn't be playing. Why not help them to help others? What if it's for a not-so-worthwhile charity? What if the money goes home with me? I'm the only charity that I know is worthwhile. How much does the American Cancer Society take for "operating expenses"?

Don't waste time coming up with reasons to justify that what you're doing is ethical. If you have a brain in your head, you can argue either way. Be okay with it, then put it behind you. Ethics only slows you down and fucks you up. If you have any qualms about taking an eighty-three-year-old's last dime, then don't take a grand off a crooked lawyer. Don't pretend that ripping off the crooked lawyer is helping society; and remember, you're more likely to get into trouble screwing the lawyer. This is not a book on how to be a hero now, is it? Would a good person buy this book? Face it—you're a scumbag.

Good people don't play poker. If you can't stand the idea of "crossing the line" into cheating, this isn't just the wrong book for you. Poker is the wrong game. There's nothing that's fair in poker. You want a fair game? Play war—there's no strategy, there's no thought, you just turn over cards. And don't play for money; that's trying to get something for nothing. Play Go Fish for fun, get a job for money. Like I said, cancer still needs a cure.

Poker is nothing but advantage. If you understand the math, you have a huge advantage over someone who doesn't. If you're good at reading people, you have a huge advantage over someone who isn't. If you've played thousands of hands, you have a huge advantage over someone who hasn't. Is that fair? Isn't it all part of the game? Do people really know what they're getting into?

Put your local high school football team in a game against the Oakland Raiders. They all know the rules. Take a fucking level to the playing field. Is it fair? No. Are the Raiders cheating? It's semantics. The end result? Someone loses.

I happen to see someone's cards because they don't protect them well. Would an honest person tell him he'd seen their cards? Sure. But an honest person wouldn't play poker and an honest person sure wouldn't win.

Lying is built into poker. Poker tells you that you're supposed to cheat. What's the difference between bluffing and lying? It's a hard question because there is no difference. Implying with your wagers that you have certain cards is no different than telling your wife that you're on a business trip when you're fucking your secretary (and if your secretary is a guy, deal with it). It's understood in the game that people can bluff. It's understood that skill levels can be all over the place. It's understood that reading a person for tells is fair and acceptable. It's part of the game. So is cheating. If they catch you, they win. If not, you win.

Not everyone is playing by the same ethical standards. The line between right and wrong is not the same for everyone, but most people assume that their ethical line is everyone's line. Once you understand that, it can help you win. People who play with friends would never cheat, and they assume that it's true for everyone they play with. It isn't.

What is cheating? Grabbing money out of the pot? What about tracking cards during the shuffle and deal? Well, that's probably cheating, but it's not as bad as grabbing chips out of the pot or dealing from the bottom of the deck. In some casinos, it's not against the rules to track cards—if it happens, it's the dealer's fault. And you won't find a casino that's never had a card mechanic doing the dealing. It's all okay.

What about fucking with people? There are a lot of players that say and do things to get in your head and put you on tilt . . . people on tilt make bad decisions, so it's a good idea to mess with their heads. It's perfectly legal in casinos. It may be impolite and frowned upon, but it's part of the game. Is it ethical to do that in a home game? Sure.

It's your turn to post a blind and you forget, but nobody notices. Do you put that money in the pot in the next hand? Does everyone you play with do the same? How can you be sure? Whatever you think is right is what's right. Winning is right.

A lot of the rules in a home game are assumed. An "advantage player" (as opposed to a cheat) doesn't want to go over the rules because, if you tell him that seeing someone else's cards by accident should be a misdeal, he'll lose his edge. The advantage player only thinks of something as being wrong when he's been directly told that it's against the rules; until then, all's fair. The cheater knows the rules and isn't fooling himself about his ethics. He knows where he stands.

Ask anyone running a home game if they've ever had someone cheating. The answer will almost always be, "No one in our game would do that!" They get indignant. These are friends, people they know and trust, and cheaters wouldn't be invited to the game. I've played in more home games than anyone you know, and I'm paying attention and I know what to look for. There's always a little cheating . . . and that adds up to a lot of cheating. Some guy "accidentally" throws fewer chips into the pot than he should. Someone else notices what the guy next to him is holding. Jokes are told that are designed to put the table on tilt. We're all friends here, but someone has to win—it might as well be you.

If I say that every game I'm in has a cheater, it wouldn't be saying much. But, in every game I'm in, I'm not the only cheater. No one would believe there's ever a cheat at the table, even though a lot of players take any advantage they can. "Why would someone cheat?" is not the real question. The real question is: Why would anyone cheat more than I cheat? Assholes.

Even in the lowest-stakes game—even when playing for no money at all—a lot of people try to get an edge. That's because people like to win. Who can blame anyone for that? The object of poker is to win, and lying and gaining unfair advantage is part of the game. You're going to push the envelope a bit past advantage play to make sure you win.

Is spotting a tell a form of cheating? Someone slams their bet down onto the table with a lot of force. All the books tell you that this means the person is bluffing, while trying to represent confidence in his betting. You notice this, so you call the bet. But, hey, maybe this person has also read the book and is trying to get you to think that they've got a weak hand when really it is strong. It's all part of the game, right? Well, it's much easier to learn tells if you know what cards a player is sitting on.

Guys wear hats and sunglasses. They don't want you to see their facial expressions or notice whether their eyes dilate. Is that cheating? If it's part of the game to read people, then why aren't sunglasses cheating? Why are they allowed to hide? Why isn't that against the rules? I don't have to read them; I dealt them the cards that I want them to have.

In poker, anything you can get away with is fair.

Some players have serious tells. A serious tell is an involuntary habit. It's the kind of thing they do in the movies, but it's rare to see it in real life. But you will. And when you find someone with a serious tell, the amount of information you get from that is staggering. I knew a guy who would smooth his hair back whenever he made a hand. It was the only time he did it, and he would do it the moment that he realized his hand was made. A straight draw on the flop, he smooths his hair back, and you know he made his straight. Would you let him know about that tell? Is that the right thing to do? If tells are a part of the game, then I've just found a really strong advantage to play. Is it fair? No hair slicking, he's bluffing; I know exactly how to bet. I tested it with a few flops that I was controlling, and then I didn't need to cheat with the cards anymore. I cheated with the person. It's safer, and it's allowed by the rules.

People think there's no "real" cheating in their home games because they assume everyone is using the same rulebook. They aren't. They trust that everyone has the same moral guidelines as they do. They don't. Trust is only questioned when it's violated. It's a trust that's made me a lot of money. Poker is not a gentleman's game.

It's either all right or it's all wrong. You can come up with a bunch of reasons for why screwing a ten-year-old hooker in the ass is a perfectly fine thing to do. If something's legal it doesn't mean it's right, and if it's illegal it doesn't mean it's wrong. Look at your fucking taxes. Remember, I don't pay taxes.

If you still think there's a line that shouldn't be crossed and that the line isn't blurry, congratulations. You passed the test. You're an ethical person. You should put down this book and sleep tonight knowing that, while some evil people may *think* about cheating, no one does it. Go to your home game and trust everyone, and I'll see you soon. I don't take checks.

Chapter 5

ADVANTAGE PLAY FOR WEASELS

I'm not the kind of guy who likes to split hairs—there's no money in it. I don't care how many angels can dance on the head of a pin unless they've got money in the pot. In that case, I suppose their money is as good as anyone's, and I hope there are plenty of them.

What is advantage play? It's cheating. It's amateur cheating, but it's cheating. They write books on it and brag about it, and people will still play with you when they catch you in advantage play, but it's still cheating. Most players think that they are allowed to use any information that comes their way. They think it's perfectly fair to notice and take advantage of the guy who licks his lips nervously like a priest at a Cub Scout meeting whenever he gets good cards. They think spotting tells makes them good players.

You're not going to limit yourself to looking for tells. Every chump and his brother has read *Caro's Book of Tells*. You'll get good at spotting tells, but you won't need to be. It's too risky to lay your money on how someone puts chips into a pot or how they're sitting in their seat. Put that power of observation into this book, and you'll see your profits go way up.

You can find a lot of books that will talk about all kinds of advantage play. You can look for nicks and smudges and memorize them. Knowing one card's location is a big advantage—not a big enough advantage for me, but an advantage. During the deal, a lot of cards get flashed. Maybe the advantage weasel won't make out every card. He doesn't have to. The easiest place to catch a glimpse of other people's cards is when they're in the blinds or when they have the dealer button on the table in front of them. Why's that? Those are the places on the table that have obstacles in front of the players, and the easiest way to deal is to toss the cards over those obstacles. A lot of dealers do this, even in the casinos. If the weasel is in the right seat, he might get a fine view. He'll also be looking at the player to his left, because getting a little peek off of him isn't hard to do.

All of this is considered fair play—unless the weasel gets caught. Of course, everything *I* do is fair play by that definition, too. I don't embarrass myself by trying to catch a glimpse. I don't sneak little peeks up short skirts—I grab the hips and fuck. When those cards are being dealt, I'm joking and looking like I'm having a good time. I'm a cheat, not a weasel. Advantage play is for weasels. If you're going to cheat, take out your cock and cheat. That's how you win.

I don't follow any rules, even my own. If it's the easiest way to get the money, I'll be a weasel. I played in a game with an annoying car salesman who couldn't stop bragging whenever he'd pull down a pot. He'd call everyone nicknames that he made up, and he'd always stand too close and spit when he talked. I was just biding my time, waiting until it was my turn to deal to take him down. But the deal went to someone else first, and that dealer gave me all I needed. I got a glimpse of the car salesman's second card on one hand—a low-value club. That's all I knew and that's all I needed. He bet big and scared everyone else out, but I stayed in. The flop came up with three diamonds. I looked him in the eye and said, "Hey, buddy, I'm sitting on a high flush, and I don't think you can beat me. I'm all-in." I had nothing and no draw, but he didn't know that. I also knew that *he* didn't have a flush (at least not yet) and I used my glimpse to bluff to a flush. It worked. Some would call that fair. I didn't get caught, so I call it fair, too.

More importantly, I didn't hurt the flow of the game. I was still sitting at the table pretending to have a good time, making jokes, being noticed when I wanted to, and not being noticed when I didn't. I was still at work. I wasn't playing little weasel games that distract me from my job. I was playing cards to win. I didn't lose sight of the game to snag a glimpse of one card.

You can stare at the dealer's hands and, a lot of the time, you'll see *paint* (a face card). Even without the exact value or suit, it's still useful information. Paint cards are worth more in poker, and knowing one card may give you a good reason to fold early. But if you follow my system, you won't have to bother with those kinds of advantage play peeks. When you need to, you'll know the cards.

Never try to grab a peek when people are looking at their cards. As a matter of fact, if the guy to your right accidentally flashes you his cards, let him know. Be on the up and up. Tell him to be careful. Cover your eyes, and reach over and tip his hand back out of your eye line. The more they trust you, the more money you make.

You do not want to get busted for a kind of cheating you don't care about. Tell them to cover up. If someone thinks you're trying to see his cards, you'll lose his trust forever and he'll always be keeping an eye on you. You don't want anyone keeping an eye on you, ever. Once you've established yourself as an honest man at the table, people will let their guard down, and that will pay off.

There's always a guy around who is trying to sneak a peek. As the cards from the last hand are mixed in, or when the deck is cut before shuffling, some lowbrow is always looking for the cards on the bottom. He'll pick one card and track where it goes through the shuffle. If it's an ace, you can track his prick getting hard in his pants. He'll watch; cards on the bottom will stay on the bottom during a riffle shuffle. A couple of shuffles and strip-cuts, and he'll still have a good idea where that card is. Let him do it. If he knows the placement of one card, he'll feel he has an advantage. You want everyone to feel like they have an advantage. People bet more when they think they have a lock. When they bet more, you win more.

Never disturb someone who's using advantage play. Let them work. Cover for them. Make small talk so they don't get noticed while they're trying to look at other people's cards. Most people are like me and don't see any difference between advantage play and cheating, and you sure don't want the table thinking about cheating. Make sure the weasel doesn't get caught. If he gets burned on it, help him. You never want that nasty word "cheating" to come up. Never. Laugh off the weasel's actions as an accident. Jump in and change the subject. Make a comment on the dealer's fine manicure.

If the weasel gets ahead at the table, it's good for you. Let him win all the other players' money at the table, then take him down yourself. If he knows that the ace of clubs is deep in the deck and then you wind up with it, he'll just think he fucked up. And if he's sure he didn't fuck up, who's he going to tell? He has to shut up. He's a weasel.

Chapter 6

PLAYING THE CARDS—YOU CAN'T BUY PRACTICE

There's no way I can give you all the information you need to become a card mechanic in one chapter. It can't be done in one book. It can't be done in any number of books. The real information is in the practice. I'll get you started and you'll buy another couple of books. Next, you've got to buy a mirror and a gross of decks of cards by every maker (everything from expensive plastic KEM-like cards to cheap shitty tourist decks). Now lock yourself in a room for several months. I'm not kidding or exaggerating. Work on one move until it becomes automatic. Don't settle for passable—each move has to be perfect. Don't get the idea in your head that you'll polish your moves at the games. It's too dangerous, and you won't get better in the games.

You have to be perfect even at 70 percent of your maximum ability. This isn't some card trick where you'll be embarrassed if you're caught. You're going to be cheating at real poker for real money. You have to be 30 percent better than perfect. You might want to invest in a video camera to film yourself straight up, and then again doing the moves so that you can compare the two. When there's no difference whatsoever between the straight version and the crooked version—from any angle—practice for another two months. Then start thinking about doing it in a real game. Think about it for maybe another two months while you practice some more. If you've never touched a deck of cards before reading this book (what kind of weird fuck buys this book when they've never even played cards?), you have a year of practice before you can cheat for money. If you're really good with cards right now, you still have a year. You need to learn everything from scratch. Get rid of all your shabby habits. You have to be clean to cheat.

You're going to have to buy some more books. I'm not going to write a lot of shit that's already been written in other places. I'm telling you how to be a cheat; other books show you how to play poker or do card moves. There's a difference. Any local magic shop will have these books. Don't buy these books at a magic shop in the same town where you're going to cheat, and don't tell the kid behind the counter that you want to learn how to cheat. If you bought the book you're reading right now in the town where you're going to cheat, that was stupid enough. You want to risk someone seeing you walking through the mall with a book on cheating? You really should buy all this cheating stuff mail order and throw away the receipts. You can't take it off your taxes anyway. You don't pay taxes.

Don't leave this book lying around. Read it and burn it. If you need it again, buy a new one (that's Dickie's marketing strategy; there's different writing on the cover, just hide the dust jacket— Penn). "Cheat" is in the title and you don't ever use the word "cheat." You're going to stop cheating on your wife; from now on you just fuck around on her. Don't think the word cheat. Never tell *anyone* you're a poker cheat.

You'll get a few books, but you absolutely have to have *The Expert at the Card Table* by S. W. Erdnase. Erdnase is a fake name for a guy who knew how to give himself a 100 percent advantage. He was a real cheat, and the book has all the real moves. *Expert* is still in print, and every magic shop and most big bookstores in the country sell it. A lot of magic books have bullshitty "poker deal" tricks—forget those. You want the basic stuff. The moves are hard, but no one has ever explained them better than Erdnase, and I'm not even going to try.

The moves you'll want to learn: all the Blind Riffles and Blind Cuts. You'll need to shuffle while keeping your top and/or bottom stock (or *slugs*) in place. Cut Locations with both crimp and jog. All the Stock Shuffles and the Cull Shuffles. "The Two-handed Erdnase Shift" (don't bother with the others—his is the best and you can use both hands most of the time). You'll need all the "Palming." All the stuff in the chapter *The Player Without an Ally* is for you, you'll never use a partner. That's it, you're done. It's a lot of reading, but it's nothing compared to the practice.

Don't bother with the Monte—that's for street punks—and you don't even want to read the *Legerdemain* section. That's for jerk-off magicians pretending they're doing what you'll really be doing. There aren't a lot of magicians who do it well, either. You're not going to be doing card tricks. The idea is to master these moves.

While you're waiting for your copy of Erdnase, here are a few things you can practice (and don't worry about the words you don't understand. After *Expert* you'll know them all):

HIT THE BRIEF

We'll start with something basic: how to *elevator the cut*. When a stacked deck needs to stay stacked, your two problems are the shuffle and the cut. You're the dealer, and you're going to do a false shuffle, so that's not a problem. But someone else is going to cut.

There are two ways you can solve the cut problem. First, you can try to force them to cut the deck exactly where you want it. Take a deck and put it in new deck order. Now cut the deck in about half. Take the lower half and put a bend in it. Put it back on the top of the deck. Go make yourself a sandwich.

Come back a few minutes later and cut the deck. Don't think about it, just do it. You'll notice that nine out of ten times you'll cut the deck back to where it was in the first place. That's because most people cut the cards the same way, and if they do it quickly, the bend in the deck makes it easy to split the pack at that point. You can practice putting that bend in while you shuffle it, so they cut it right back to where it was. Put in enough of a bend that it works, but not enough that it's noticed.

Another way to get them to cut where you want is to give the cards a last cut, then sprinkle a few grains of salt from your pretzel on top of the cards before giving it to them for their cut. You get the cards in the order you want, you cut the deck (with the salt on top), and you hand it to another player to cut. The salt separates the two halves just a little bit, just like a dog-ear in a book makes it fall open to that page. Their cut puts it back the way you want it. You've read this—you think you got it? No way. You have to practice. Yup, you have to practice bending cards just right and flicking salt from your pretzel. Believe me, it still beats working for a living.

SHIFTING

The other way to take care of the cut is to let the other player cut the deck fairly, then do a *pass* (or a *shift*) to put it back. A pass is basically a cut done in your hands, but it's done very fast and under cover so no one sees it. If you've got a new deck, you can square it up perfectly by pinching the sides. Let someone cut it. Most people will grab half the pack and slap it down, and then it won't line up perfectly. You'll be able to lift up a corner of the bottom card of the top packet and jam your pinky in there. Right when you're going to do the move ask someone a question. Make sure it's a real question. If you ask, "What's the blind?" every time you do the pass, it'll start to look fishy. Think of your question before you pick up the cards and be ready to time what you say with the move. Pull down on your pinky, raise the lower half up and around the top half, and presto—the deck is back in the order it was in when you started. This is the granddaddy of all cheat moves. People work on the shift their whole lives. Erdnase will give you more, but no words can really help; the shift takes a lot of practice. Books will get you started, mirrors and film will let you work alone, but mostly it takes thousands of hours of practice.

There are other ways to force the cut. You can do it by putting a step in the deck; it's amazing how often people will cut the deck to the right place. And if you get a smart-ass who deliberately under- or over-cuts the deck, don't forget that cutting the deck doesn't fuck up the order. Your jog or saddle will still be there, and you can do a pass to put things where you need them. You have to practice what to do when people fuck you. Practice until you don't care if they cut in the wrong place. Practice it until nothing can fuck you.

Many home games now use a "cut card." It's not hard to get around—just hold a break and slide the cut card in right there. As you practice, you'll feel it.

SHUFFLING, BUT NOT REALLY

There's a lot written on false shuffles, but what you need is the *false riffle shuffle*. Poker people don't usually use an *overhand shuffle* (bridge players use that a lot), but you'll want to have a good false overhand along with your false riffle.

For an easy overhand shuffle, hold the deck by the sides (that's the long sides), and pull a packet off the top and into your other hand. Keep doing that, grabbing clumps of cards. As you get down to the last few cards, pull them off one by one. This is a good way to move cards from the bottom of the pack to the top. This just moves your top stock to the bottom and mixes up the rest of the cards.

False riffles range from stupidly easy to impossible. (The ones I do are impossible.) The best technique to start with is to do a few riffles at an angle where you can see the cards on the bottom. When you see a card you want (like an ace), keep it on the bottom by splitting the cards so that it's always on the same side. Just make it fall first in the shuffle. Later on, you'll shuffle it from the left side to the right side, making it hard to tell where it is.

Let's say there's an ace on the bottom of the deck. Split the deck in half and get ready to riffle them together. The ace is now on the bottom of the pack in your right hand. You let the cards riffle together, but you let the cards in your right hand fall first, so that the ace is still on the bottom. You can do this as many times as you want. Try putting the pack with the ace on the bottom in your left hand and letting those cards fall first. Do ten shuffles, ace on the bottom in the left hand, ace on the bottom in the right hand. Ten wasn't bad, was it? Now do another ten thousand.

As you riffle, look into the packets for other aces. When you see one, try to remember where it is in the deck. Split the pack at that point (it doesn't matter if the two halves are unequal). If you get it (and you'll get better with practice), you'll wind up with a packet in each hand with an ace on the bottom. Interweave the two bottom cards and let the rest mix together. Now you've got two aces on the bottom. You're getting the idea. After 100,000 of these shuffles it won't be an idea anymore—it'll be part of you.

At the end of the riffles, you can use an overhand shuffle to put the two aces on top (along with a few more indifferent cards,) so you have a *stack*. You can also leave them on the bottom and deal from the bottom. Or, you can do an overhand shuffle where you hold the deck in your left hand and pull two cards into your right: the top and bottom card. You keep pulling packets of two cards, putting them beneath the first cards pulled off. If there are two aces on the bottom of the deck, you'll pull a random card, followed by an ace, followed by another random card, followed by the other ace. If you shuffle them off to the top and deal them (heads up), you'll get the aces. If you repeat this process, you'll get set up with enough random cards for as many players as are at the table.

Stacking the deck at the table by using shuffles sounds a lot harder than it turns out to be when you practice it a few times. But doing it right is much harder than it seems after the first few hours. It should take you less than twenty seconds to set up the cards you want during the shuffle. Any longer, and people will wonder why you're spending so much time shuffling. You don't have to go through the deck completely, and you can mix up your shuffling styles, but it has to be perfect and natural.

There are a couple of shuffles that you won't use for stacking; one is the *pull-through*. That's basically a riffle shuffle, but after the cards are weaved together, you push them together at a little angle so that you can separate them again. You can do that during the waterfall or without the waterfall, but whatever you do, you'll have to match it in all your shuffles. You must *always* shuffle the same.

DEALING FROM ANYWHERE

Dealing seconds takes longer to master than anything else. It's got a few advantages over dealing from the bottom. Bottom dealers have to worry about accidentally flashing the bottom card. *Hangers* are common. Bottom dealing *talks* more than second dealing (it makes the wrong noise). You can get around a lot of this by being careful. The talking problem can be taken care of by working on getting the same sound from dealing from the top. You have to snap the cards onto the table harder than you would with a normal deal. Once you learn to do it, you have to relearn your normal deal to make it sound like your bottom deal. Dealing seconds or bottoms works better in games of five people or fewer, because you won't have to do a long toss across a big table to reach the players out of your reach.

When you deal from the bottom, you start by getting into a little rocking motion: Your hands swivel in and out a bit as you peel the card off the top. In reality, your index finger is grabbing it from the bottom and sliding it up and out along the sides. The rocking of the deck and the bottom card helps hide the fact that it's coming out too low. It has to look perfect. Is it looking good? Do it a million more times.

Second dealing looks a bit more natural. You slide the top card out with the thumb holding the deck, as your dealing hand gets close. Just as your dealing thumb gets to the deck, you pull the top card back so your thumb catches the second card and slides it out. The big problem with dealing seconds is that you're only controlling that one card. Sometimes that's enough. Other times, you'll want a full stack at the bottom that you can use whenever you need it.

Some people say that you can only deal seconds or bottoms with a new deck because the cards slide over each other much more easily. That's not true. Any deck can be underdealt. That why you have a gross of each kind, and that's why you don't throw them away when they get worn out. You have to be able to do all your moves with old beat-up decks, too.

I met a guy in the Southwest who claimed he could deal from

the middle of the pack. Why bother? You probably don't even need to learn both seconds and bottoms at first; get good at one or the other and you'll make wages every time you play. I only learned both because I wanted more options and I like to practice. It's peaceful to me. It's something I can do when I watch television that will earn me money. Any move you know will come in handy in a game at some point. Sometimes players know about basement dealing. Fine—flash them the bottom card as you deal seconds.

The disadvantage of second dealing is that you often need to do a back peek. Squeeze the sides of the deck to bow the top card up a little so you can get a glimpse. Make sure the deck is tipped up; otherwise players opposite you can see the bowing. When your nail nicking gets good, most of the time you won't need the peek. You can get all your information before you touch the deck.

When you deal from the bottom, always think about hangers (cards out of alignment with the deck). If you rock your hands a bit, you'll be able to see a hanger and fix it before anyone notices. Don't get sloppy. Hangers happen to even the best mechanics in the world, but if you're aware of them, you can make sure no one sees them. If you get into the habit of casually dropping your deck hand on the table during pauses in the deal, you can use that move to square up the hanger.

PALM BEATING

Being able to palm a card flawlessly does have one requirement: You can't have tiny hands. You don't need bear paws, but if you can't completely cover a card with your hand, you can't palm a card. Maybe poker cards are the size they are to keep women, children, and dwarves out of the card-cheating business. My hands aren't great for palming, either—so many of my fingers have been broken over the years that they don't line up too good, and I've got big windows between the fingers. Even so, I learned to overlap them in a way that you can't see between them. It looks natural because I have my hand in that position even when I'm not cheating (and that's not much of the time, by the way). I used to practice holding my hands like that all the time. Now, it's my natural position. I jerk off with my fingers overlapping.

The best way to lay a palm beat on someone is to get a premium card on top of the deck. After the deal, as you're putting down the cards, palm the top card. Keep it there. See if it helps your hand. If it does (and it almost always will), you can make the switch for one of your hole cards, then dump your deadwood to the top of the deck as you pick it up to deal the flop. That card becomes a burn card, anyway. The other option is to keep that good card on top of the deck, palm it off as you deal the burn card, and deal it to the board whenever it helps you most.

Say you've got pocket rockets preflop. You've stashed another ace on top of the deck. The betting is fat. You palm off the ace, burn a card, deal out a flop. Put the ace back on the deck. The betting gets higher. You grab the deck, palm off the ace again, burn a card, and deal the turn. Return the ace again. More betting. Final round, you palm off the ace, burn a card, return the ace to the top, and deal the ace on the river. You've got three aces. By holding on to it, you've jacked up the pot a lot more than you would have if you'd shown it right off the bat on the flop.

You can put a palm beat on players in twist games on almost every hand. I like to keep a block of high cards on the bottom of the deck when I deal. I swap them out for my palmed card whenever I need them.

If you've got some action with a chump in the baker's seat, flash him one of your hole cards. Make it look like an accident, but don't say anything. Now bet into him with a little bit of cocky needling. And if—rather than politely telling you that he accidentally saw your card—he raises you? Wait till he goes for his chips, then use the shade to swap the hole card that you flashed him for one that helps your hand. When he loses, he'll have a tough time convincing any-one that you cheated, especially if you put your deadwood back into the deck. If he calls you out, start by asking him why he thinks you cheated. If he admits he saw your card, he'll be the shit-eater, espe-cially when you ask him what card he thought you had. Ask every-one if the card is in play; no one will have it. Have someone look through the stub; when they find it buried in the middle, he'll look like a fool. More than likely, though, he'll never say anything, and he'll figure that he misread the card he saw when you flashed him.

HOLDING OUT

There are a lot of mechanical contraptions that people use for holding out cards. I've seen some crazy gadgets, but I stay away from any of that kind of breastwork. Sometimes they fail (or get hung up on your clothes) and—worse than that—if you get busted with a *spider,* you're going to have a tough time convincing anyone that you have no idea how it got on you. Some guys make their whole living with a *lizard* and I can use one pretty well, but I've spent tens of thousands of hours practicing. It'll give you a very clean game and lots of control, but I don't like being that dirty if I get nabbed. If you want to put in the time, a hold-out's a great gadget; it's just not my style.

The closest thing to a hold-out device that I'll use is a kind of *bug.* I'll get that blue putty they make for putting posters up on a wall. It doesn't leave any sticky residue and it's great for sticking your hold-outs to the bottom of the table. It will leave a grease spot after a few weeks. I found that out after forgetting about a card I left on the bottom of a game table—until I came back for another game a month later. I felt it under the table, lapped it, and decided to use it. I brought it into play in the new game and noticed a slight color change on the face. No one else saw it, fortunately. That was the day that I learned not to drink so much that I forget where I've stashed my deadwood. It's a lesson you should learn. Squirrels forget where they leave their stash and we get oak trees; if you forget, you might wind up hanging from one.

In a pinch, you can stash your hold-out cards just about any-where. I've heard of guys hiding hold-outs under an ashtray, but I don't. People sometimes grab ashtrays and move them, and that could be bad. The gap between the table and the bumper on the bottom of a real poker table will work. Every kind of table has a place underneath to hide a card. You might want to go to Goodwill and pick up a couple of different kinds of tables. As your games get richer and you start playing with people that have nice (expensive) poker tables, you'll have to buy one to practice on, but you'll have the money by the time that happens. I also like to keep cards under my leg but you have to be careful because the cards do get notice-ably warm under there. If you're holding out under your leg or in your lap, you can't forget it's there, in case you need to stand up un-expectedly. Maybe the host's wife comes home and everyone stands up to greet her. Having a cascade of court cards fall out of your lap will raise the eyebrows of even the dumbest of dumb asses.

Once you've got your deadwood, you'll want to get it away from you as soon as you can. Don't rush it. You never want to have more than seven cards out of play—more than that and you risk an average player noticing the difference in the thickness of the deck. I can tell if a deck is light by even a single card. I can also tell if the deck is heavy by a card. Most people can't do that, but seven is the limit before an average player will see that something is wrong.

You want to stay away from adding cards from a duplicate deck. It's too risky. In a nine-handed game of Hold 'Em, there will be twenty-three cards in play. If you swap in an extra ace of spades, there's almost a 50 percent chance that someone has that ace that hand. Just be patient and the cards you need will eventually fall into your lap (literally).

A great time to unload deadwood is during the *wash*. Palm them all and when a stray card is pushed toward you during the wash, add your cards to the mix as you push it back to the center of the table.

SLUGS

Since most people won't notice fewer than seven cards missing from the deck, I make a point of grabbing six or seven before my deal, lapping them, and waiting for the deal to come around to me. When I'm out of the action, I'll drop one hand into my lap and see what I've got. Out of six or seven cards, you'll always find something that will guarantee a winning pot. In Texas Hold 'Em, that's another three and a half possible hands. In other games, that's another full hand. It more than doubles your chances of "getting lucky" because you can mix and match. Never drop both hands to check out those cards. Don't stare in your lap too long. I like to keep my other hand on my drink and take a few sips. Glance down, put some cards in order, glance up. You're out of the action when this is happening, so no one should be paying attention to you, but stay alert.

When I have a six- or seven-card slug, I'll just add it to the bottom after the cards have been shuffled and cut. Then I'll get them into play with bottom dealing. I'll arrange for them to be used as my hole cards, or the flop, or someone else's hole cards, depending on what I need.

COLD DECKING

Ice is a powerful tool for any crossroader. Once you learn to *ring in* your cold deck, you'll be able to boost pots higher than you ever imagined. This is more powerful when you know your sheep—even tight players will go all-in when they are sitting on a monster hand.

First of all, the reason they're called "cold decks" is because when you play with a deck for a while, it feels warmer compared to a deck that hasn't been in play. I've never had anyone notice the difference, but to be safe, I like to keep all my decks warm. A jacket pocket works very well . . . too much body heat and the cards will feel too warm (which I have seen people notice).

There are a lot of clever methods for deck switching. I use several because I do a lot with stacks. Over the years, I've turned to ringing in half-stacks because it avoids the problem of ever having two full decks (or no full decks) on the table. The key is to create the impression that the deck is on the table the whole time. I might keep a single card from the real deck, held the same way I'd hold a full deck—tilted at an angle so you can't tell that it's only a single card. Then I go to my lap, grab the ice, and slide it under the top card. I now have one extra card that I palm off and drop on top of the real deck in my lap. I'll also do full-out switches; usually I'll palm my cold deck and reach across to get a drink. My arm acts as a shield to cover the real deck. As I'm getting my drink with my right hand, my left hand puts the stacked deck in front of another player to cut. As my hand pulls back, I slide the real deck into my lap. A little choreography goes a long way. He cuts the stack at the crimp (or I undo the cut), and I'm ready to go.

The next thing to talk about is building a good stack. I played in a game with a fellow we'll call Pug. I set it up so that no one would get playable cards. Pug was the big blind and he was dealt J-6. I gave myself Q–10. I limped in and he checked; everyone else folded. If Pug had made a bigger bet to steal the blinds, I would've called.

The flop, turn, and fifth street brought a double belly-buster draw: J–8–7–5–9. Pug stayed in after the flop because he had top pair. Because I limped into the pot, he wasn't worried that I had a higher pair, and I did nothing but call or make the minimum bets. When he saw the turn, he bet a little bigger because he had an open-ended straight draw and top pair. On the river, Pug made his nine-high straight. He checked and I bet big, which he called. If he'd bet big, I would've raised him, and he'd have had a tough time not calling. Pug would have been hard-pressed to put me on Q–10 (which is the only hand that could beat him), but because he had cards just good enough to stay in (until the river), my play made perfect sense to him in hindsight. I got him all-in and made two large on that one hand. Being stacked can make you money. Just ask Ann-Margret.

Most guys can't lay down a straight, and my queen-high straight beat his jack-high straight. Another good scenario for a stack is a flush that's made on the river. I give my friend A–10. The flop comes 4h–10c–10s. He's sitting on three of a kind with an ace kicker and he bets big. I call each round of betting. The turn is a Qs, which doesn't hurt him. The river is a 6s. Boy, is he surprised when I show my 4s–3s and win with a spade flush. Until the river, I had a pair of fours. He walks away having lost a mint, and he's convinced that I'm a really weak player who got lucky and sucked out.

Be smart when you pick your stack. You want them to lose just barely, and usually through a bad beat on the turn or river. Don't cripple the deck. If you give yourself a pair of bullets and the flop shows the two other aces, you won't drum up much action (unless it's from someone bluffing an ace). If you have to turn up that hand and you've got four aces, there will be a lot of suspicious looks when they see your white blackbird. Make the hands believable and not impossibly lucky.

Here's another example: Give good preflop hands to five players at the table and keep a weak hand like 4–5 suited for yourself. Say your opponents get: A–Q, K–K, K–K, A–J, A–10. All monsters. They'll all bet big preflop. You stay in. The flop comes J–3–10. That's a great hand for everyone, and they should all stay in. The turn is a 6. Again, no one should worry that they're beat except for maybe the guy with A–10. Because of all the action preflop, everyone is expecting monster hands like A–A, but the bets will settle down after the flop. The river brings a 7. The two guys with pocket kings should stay in all the way, believing their kings are good. The guy with A–J has top pair with his fishhooks, and A–10 has second pair with the best kicker. Mr. A–Q has the inside nut straight draw. In the end, though, your lowly 4–5 makes you the winner with a runner-runner 7-high straight.

I've used that stack a number of times: You'd think the players would see the cards after the showdown and think something was up. They remember the hand because of all the paint, but it never seems to strike anyone as suspicious. That's because none of the hands ever came very close to winning. The key is that no one hand was a super monster hand: an unlikely number of players had good cards, but no one made anything higher than a straight. Weird, but not impossible. Players only get suspicious when you win with a premium hand like four of a kind or a straight flush.

Obviously, you don't want to set up your stacks to have one four of a kind get beaten by a higher four of a kind. A straight losing to a flush, or a flush losing to a full house works well.

On occasion I like to ring in half a cold deck. With nine players, you need two hole cards each, three burn cards, three cards for the flop, and one each for fourth and fifth street. That's twenty-six cards for one round. I make two twenty-six-card half-stacks and ring them in one half at a time. With practice, you can cut a deck exactly in half every time (there's that damn practice thing again). During my shuffle, I grab the top half of the real deck and swap in the top half of the stack. After the hand, I swap in the second half of the cold deck, gather the used half, and put it on top. I swap out the cold deck (the bottom half of which is still prepared) and swap in the real deck, then shuffle and deal again. When the deal comes back to me, I take the fresh part of the cold deck and use it, then bring it out of play. This is a bit risky if you lose control of the deck for any reason. It does give you twice as much bang for your cold-deck buck, though. You're going to have to practice.

You may be tempted to learn every card move you can find. You don't need a hundred ways to do a pass. You need one way that you can do perfectly, 100 percent of the time. You have to be a lot better than good. Being perfect 99 percent of the time is good, but do you really want to see what happens during the 1 percent of the time you fuck it up?

Avoid the Hollywood bullshit. Don't do any Charlier Passes or one-handed shuffles. Why would you want anyone at the table to know how hard you've worked on your card manipulations? You're much better off having them think that you've never held a card before in your life. Cheating will make you money, but it won't let you show off. If you want to show off, buy a big TV and a fancy car and wow the girls.

This brings up another issue. Never do magic tricks. You'll want to learn a couple because it will help you perfect your moves, but no one should ever see you do them. And never bank on the idea that someone you meet at the supermarket is someone who will never see you again. In small towns, no one is safe, because you don't know who they know. You can't even do card tricks for hookers. Let them do the tricks. Keep your secret powers to yourself, Superman.

That being said, you want a couple of good tricks that use sleights. You want to have those down just in case you ever get busted doing a move. With the right crowd (a crowd that's been tuned into your personality as a laid-back, fun guy) you can laugh off the fact that you got busted cheating by doing a couple of quick tricks, and then return all the chips you won through your shifty (and shitty, since you got caught) moves. Tell your friends that you needed a friendly environment just to put your skills to the test— you'd *never* keep their money. As a show of good faith, you won't deal for the rest of the night. You never want to use this plan—it's not a good solution. But if you get busted big time—for example, when a palmed ace falls out of your supposedly empty hand—it could work. Denying everything works great unless there's hard evidence lying on the felt. "I was just kidding around" is a marginally better defense than nothing. You can make it stronger by keeping a couple of business cards with your magic name on them. I suggest "The Amazing Hamhand."

Chapter 7

WHY HOME GAMES?

Once you learn all the mover's skills, you can earn a living in any kind of game. So why cheat home games and not work over the tourists in the casinos? Why not go to the hundreds of mitt joints across the country?

First off, flat games are filled with risks. You'll find plenty of action where they won't care if you play crooked, but you'll get the sweet crap beaten out of you by other grifters who won't want you muscling in on their action.

Home games are ripe for the picking. There are more George games going on in a bullshit town than you'll ever find at the swankiest casino in Vegas. A lot of people would rather blow their money in their weekly payday game than spend a bundle on tickets and hotels to get to the closest casino. If they stay home, they have more money to play with and more to lose to you. Why should you split your money with Wayne Newton?

There are pros and cons (other than you) in the home game. First, you'll have to play with a lot of idiots. Don't let them frustrate you. Many of them won't know the game. Almost every single one of them will believe that they're a "much better than average" player. They'll try to be hip and act like riverboat gamblers. One guy I played with proudly showed his pocket aces and announced that he had "US Air" instead of "American Airlines" (A-A). They'll make you sick because they're so stupid and so easily taken. Don't get cynical. They're like children. Be patient and support them. Children aren't smart; they're little robots that do and feel what you teach them to do and feel. Unlike children, home game players won't give you their love, they'll only give you their money. And that's better any day.

The rules are more relaxed in home games. You'll often get wacky rule variations that make cheating even easier. Take non-standard hands like pelter, blaze, Dutch straights, big cats, around the corner straights, skeet, etc. No real card room plays with these, but in home games they're very common. These hands are often harder to spot on the board, and a lot of players forget about them. You'll know the odds of hitting them, too—they won't. (For you, the odds of hitting your hand will always be 100 percent.)

A lot of people play with rules designed to get the pots sweeter faster, like *No Gypsy,* where the minimum bet is twice the big blind, or *Rangdoodles,* where the limits go up after a premium hand shows. Some people like to play with double or triple rangdoodles, but you don't want to push a pot beyond double rangdoodles. That's too unlikely to happen without cheating and someone might notice.

Many players like to add a twist (optional card) to their game at home; the players that have never heard of it are usually willing to try it. It's very popular since it leads to more interesting hands. It's also easier to cheat in hands with optional cards in play because you've only got to get one card on top of the deck (and you can have someone else deal it to you, even if you're deep into the hand).

Some home games will try to have an ax (a rake or a drop). Anyone running one of these games is trying to rip off his friends because he's making money off of every hand whether he plays or not. He's trying to run his own little casino in Dogfuck, Indiana.

Why should he get to keep the vig? If he has a drop box built into the table, you should feel free to take any opportunity to pry that fucker open and keep the contents for yourself—but wait until you're ready to *burn* that game and move on. If you keep a *slammer* with you (that's a long flat rod covered with adhesive), you can take money out of the drop and still come back the next week. When no one's looking, you jam it around in the drop box, and cash and chips will stick to it. Peel it off and go fishing again. No one keeps track of how much should be in there, so no one will know if money's missing.

The casual game is great, too, because you can get a lot more mileage out of using *hoops* and *blocks* for collateral with friends. There are hustlers who try to peddle that crap in card rooms but, for the most part, people are on to those scams there. In home games, though, when you offer up a precious family heirloom as collateral on a loan, they'll give you more for it, and probably expect that you'll buy it back eventually. There's not much in life that's more satisfying than getting a chump to loan you $500 on a five-dollar ring, then using that stake to clean out both him and his friends. Friends are also a lot more likely to give you credit and never ask about the markers. That would be so very rude among friends, don't you think?

Friendly poker games aren't rigid about their rules on table stakes, either. You can reach into your pockets for more money whenever you want—everyone knows each other and why wouldn't you allow that? You won't ever go digging, but everyone else at the table will. You'll be surprised by how many people will bring out their tough money in a home game. Regular players rarely get hit hard on any given night so, when they do, they'll probably expect to

win next time around. If they go down big (and they will), they figure their luck will change. In casinos and card rooms, most players
have a budget and some will stick to it. The psychology of the home
game makes it easier to bring out the money that "can't be touched."
It's just between friends, right? Other people's "nest eggs" are my retirement money. I had a minnow go deep for five large in one night
when he only planned to play for a nickel. That's satisfying.

Your exposure on any given night is limited because you won't
get shaken down even in the unlikely event that you fuck up and
get caught or lose. Often, they just make you leave and never come
back. There's no professional muscle in a home game. In a casino,
there are punishment professionals waiting around to fuck you up
so bad that your great-great-grandkids will be born with limps.

There's a lot more gravy in home games, including: side bets,
snacks, booze (that isn't watered down), big (unattended) kitties,
and lonely housewives who are often neglected for cards. Be nice to
the wives, and they'll be nice to you. Lend them your ear, and they'll
lend you their pussies.

Being a nice guy doesn't pay off in other places, but in home
games it's worthwhile. What card room will let you sit down with
no money (or credit) to your name? In homes, your friends will often let you go cow with them for the buy-in. If you want to make a
big bet but didn't bring much cash, they'll offer you lights. It's
friendly, so it's not "about the money." I find it personally satisfying
to walk into a game where, thanks to the kindness of everyone at
the table, I'm able to win a big dime in one night without ever
showing more than twenty dollars. That's a 500 to 1 return.

You can give a little bit back in home games. Don't be afraid of
some complimentary play to keep everyone having fun. You'd tip a
dealer in a casino, so why not give a little (very little, of course)
back to your friends? Offer to chop pots once in a while before the

showdown; you'll always have the winning hand when you offer, and when someone takes you up on it, you'll only be winning half the pot. It throws people off the cheating scent. You lose out on half of some pots, but the upside is that you'll have to show fewer winning hands when you chop with another player. When someone playing against you is bluffing, they'll be relieved and you won't have to turn over yet another winning hand.

Make a point of always losing drink pots. You want to be the guy who somehow always seems to be buying the drinks. Even though it's "loser pays," people remember you as a good sport, and people are very happy to have their drinks paid for. Keep them happy and they'll come back.

Generally speaking, card rooms are filled with savvy players. Casinos get a strange mix (depending upon the casino) of tourists and pros. Home games are always much easier to get a read on. There's a lot less variance in the play, and home games attract players who all have the same style. Friends don't like to play with people who play differently than they do; they want similar skill levels and similar styles, and that's what you give them (with a little something extra).

Tight players at home games are better than the loose tourists you'll find in the casinos (unless they're sexy coeds on spring break—but there's pussy in middle America, too). Loose players lose their poke and quit; they also get fed up easily. High breeze hummers are easier to clean out because when they get the good cards, they'll bet big.

The home game offers a lot more screen-outs to cover your dirty work: wives, music, kids running around, phone calls, pizza delivery, neighbors, and sports on TV all add up to create a constant distraction for other players. You'll find a lot of guys looking out the window during a long game.

Home game players are more likely to have their noses wide open after a bad play because they're playing with their friends. After a mistake, they feel like they have to save face. They get embarrassed and ribbed, and that puts them further on tilt. This makes it easier to cheat them, too. . . . Players on tilt make bad decisions, but they're predictably bad decisions that you can capitalize on.

Unlike in casinos or card rooms, there's not much turnover in home games. You beat a guy in a card room and he'll get up and leave. People will stick around all night in home games, which gives you a lot more time to get all of their money.

In casinos you might run into a card mob that's working a table. They can get pissed if you horn in on their action. I've sat at tables with eight sharks and one minnow. Let them take turns snacking on chum; you have bigger fish to fry in the heartland.

Casinos and card rooms are loaded with players who know enough about cheating to fuck you; these pipe salesmen are less likely to rat you out at a home game because you've been vouched for by someone else in order to get into the game. No one wants to insult another guy's friend. Social pressure works in your favor.

You want to work home games. A top poker professional stands to win, on average, a few hundred grand a year—but they'll have good years and bad years. You cheat at home games and you can clear half a million every year you choose to work. And you won't have to worry about bad years.

Chapter 8

HOW TO MAKE YOUR HOME POKER GAME CHEAT PROOF

The editor said that to sell this book, there had to be a chapter on how to protect your friendly home game from being walked over. Now you can feel better about being in the middle of reading a book meant for "bad people." Sucker.

1) Always use standard playing cards with a white border.

Bicycle, Tally-Ho, Kem, or similar brands are good choices. You want a quality card with a white border. The white border makes it more difficult for the cheater to deal seconds.

2) Regularly swap decks in play.

Any player should be able to call for a deck switch at the start of a new hand, and that should be explained to all players. You should always have two decks at the card table, each with a different color back.

3) All shuffling should be done in full view of all the players.

There is never any reason for a deck to be shuffled in someone's lap. With several pairs of eyes on the shuffling process, it will be harder for a cheat to manipulate the cards.

4)   Keep all money in a small lockbox away from the table.

This will avoid confusion when players buy-in or cash-out, and the money won't get mixed in with the chips.

5)   Only play for big money with people you like, or who have good references that you trust.

When games become about the money and not about friendship, there is a much greater temptation for people to cheat. Be a good judge of character, and don't play with people you don't trust.

6)   If extra cards are found on or around a player that you suspect might have been cheating, it is not just the host's responsibility to confront that person, it's everyone's responsibility.

Never jump to conclusions, but calmly try to find out what really happened. Don't encourage violence, but don't be afraid to stop inviting a player back if you have good and sufficient reason to suspect he's cheating. Make sure you're only playing with people you trust.

7)   The host of a game is not beyond reproach.

Just because someone is hosting the game doesn't mean that they aren't cheating. What if they set up the game for that purpose? The host of the game has the cards and the chips, and he knows the room. If you think someone is cheating, don't rule out the host.

8)   Keep all items on the table. You don't want hands to disappear from view.

Use cup holders if you're worried about spills and big ashtrays if you're worried about cigarette or cigar burns. You don't want players constantly reaching for drinks or lighters in places where no one can see what they're doing.

9) Play only with chips—don't allow cash on the table.

Cash games encourage temptation. Buying chips allows you to keep track of how much everyone has put in and taken out. In the event that the play of the game has been fouled up, you can at least give everyone back what they started with. Cash games are harder to keep track of.

10) Be aware of pairs of players who talk to each other a lot.

Two players who are constantly chatting (and winning) might be working together. Watch for signals or unusual phrases that are repeated. If two players seem to be working together, you can suggest that people reduce their table talking. You can periodically ask people to switch seats.

There's your fucking list. Memorize it.

Now here's how to get around every item on that list. Maybe someone flips through this book in the bookstore and, because they're too cheap to buy the book, they just look at the list. They're saving their scratch for poker. Good for them. Here's where you take advantage of the cheapskates. They may see that list and a couple of things may stick with them, and that's great; I love half-smart.

First of all, the playing cards don't make a mound of shit's worth of difference. It's true that the red backs (like Bee cards) are easier to deal seconds with, but not much. If your second is so sloppy that you need the extra cover, you'll get busted by Stevie Wonder on the sound alone. You're not ready to use that technique in a game. If you palm cards off the bottom of the deck, a solid red background doesn't flash as much as a white border against your skin, but why the fuck would you palm off the bottom? White borders are more help than hurt. Put a corner crimp in a card without a border and it's easier to notice; the white border helps hide it. Same is true for nicking and pegging. Also, when you wash the cards, cards with borders are much easier to track on the table. Spread this rule around. We want them to use cards with borders.

Regularly swapping decks makes people feel like they're stopping the cheat in his tracks. They'll swap, but not for new decks. They'll swap between two decks and think they're safe. Your work won't go away. You prep one deck over several hands, they swap. You prep that deck and wait for them to swap again so your work is back in play. Let them switch their asses off. You can hold out cards from the red deck and sit on them. Cards won't go bad. You don't want to put cards from a blue deck into play with a red deck, obviously, but I've done it in a pinch; the idea is to win, not color-coordinate. You can leave marks, crimps, steps, and any other work in a deck until they swap back. As a matter of fact, most people play with the same decks for weeks, or even years. You can set up your game, and have that work as long as you're in the game, with no one noticing.

You have to do all your shuffling in front of the players. Let them stare at your shuffling. That's why you practiced. What will they see? Nothing, if you do it right, and you better be doing it right. I've seen guys try to load a deck during a shuffle by trying to cover up. If you're out in the open, no one will watch. If you want a little smoke, talk while you shuffle. When you talk, people watch your eyes. Don't burn your own hands. You'll have to glance down to spot cards, but if you want to watch how good you are, watch in the mirror at home and then you can jerk off, too, if you have to.

Keeping money in a lockbox away from the table is good because you want everyone to think their money is secure. They shouldn't let a worry cross their little minds. You'll know where the lockbox is; it won't be hidden because it's locked. The banker and the players will need to get at that money, but the further away it is from the table, the better. If it's out of sight, you can stop by and make withdrawals during piss breaks—if you're the first one to cash out, you can be home before they notice any shortage. When you're leaving town and it's time to burn a game, you just leave the room when you're not playing, take the whole box, and call it quits for the evening. Remember, they're playing for fun, and they'll still have that. You're playing for money, and when it's right, take the money and split.

Playing only with people you like or people that have good references makes your life easier. You'll only be playing with people who like you. If you can't manage being well-liked, you can't cheat. You need the suckers' trust, and if people like you, they'll trust you. Your poker friends will refer you to other games because they like you. Poker is just about money, but no one wants to admit that. You want people to be at ease in big-money games. Everyone should like each other, but most of all everyone should like you.

The tip about confronting a cheat in a group is helpful to you, too. You'll never have deadwood found on or near you. Get your unwanted cards back in the deck where they belong or, if there are a lot of eyes on you, ditch them on someone near you. You'll join the witch hunt when someone else finds a two of hearts under another guy's seat. Then, in the confusion of everyone yelling at one poor asshole who has no idea what's going on, you can slip out. Slip out in a huff. If you're the one who gets busted (you lousy fuck-up), having a group of guys confront you makes it less likely that one guy will get violent right away. It's more confusing. They have to organize and you'll be glad for the cover. But you aren't going to get caught. If you do, don't mention that you read this book, okay?

Have everyone worry about the host, because you'll never be the host. "My place is too small and I have young kids, a meth lab, and a dead body in the freezer; you wouldn't want to go over there." This is one case where you might not be lying. It probably will be too small (the kids, meth lab, and dead body are your business). You'll be on the move a lot. If you do work in one town for a while, you won't want anyone to know where you live. There's no reason to risk having anyone stop by in the middle of the night with a baseball bat. If you're ever accused (you sloppy loser), you should point out that it's the host's cards and chips. They can't prove that the host wasn't cheating, and that can be the end of the discussion.

People are fussy about having drinks or ashtrays on the table because people get drunk and spill. And if you have a real card table, it might be expensive and you won't want to get it all fucked up. If you keep a lot of shit on the table, you've got more things you can use as distractions. Knock over a drink. Ditch a card under a big ashtray. Your lighter can be used as a shiner. You'll still be able to move cold decks, slugs, and hold-outs on and off the table, and clutter will help.

Playing with chips is much better. Chips are easier to cop. People never watch chips the same way they watch cash. Put a stack of centuries on the felt and people (rich or poor) will be staring. That's cash money. It commands attention. Even a fin will have people looking at the pot. When there's thousands of dollars in cash in a pot, people are watching everything, but chips are just play money. People bet more with chips because chips feel meaningless.

To suggest that two players might be working together to cheat is not all that bright, but *you* try to pull ten fucking rules out of your ass. You don't want anyone to think about cheating, ever. But if they're going to think about cheating, you want them to think about team cheating, because you'll never be in a team. The cheese stands alone.

I can give you lists all day and night. But if you want to make sure you don't get cheated at poker, either don't play poker or be the one that's cheating. There is no such thing as a cheat-proof game.

Chapter 9

FINDING GAMES

When you're cheating, you're going to burn bridges like Sherman. Don't let that get you down. It means nothing. It'd be true if you won fair and square. The same group of guys wouldn't take to losing week after week after week, even if everything was kosher. People don't like to lose. They like it less and less every week that you beat them without a break. Maximize your wins and move on.

You're doing the losers a favor. If you beat them straight, they'll lose interest in a game they enjoy. Instead of winning a little bit of money for several months, you can clean them out quick in a few sessions. You're saving them frustration. You'll also scare out the guys that shouldn't be playing anyway—like the guy who can't afford to lose. If any of this helps you sleep better at night, then go ahead and believe it. But if cheating is going to bother you, shouldn't you have bought a book on cigars? Those are popular now, too.

You can't cheat without a game, so a big part of your job is finding the games. You've got to constantly make new best friends and put yourself in pleasant contact with people who are likely to play cards for decent money. Cheating for pennies or pretzels won't make the price of this book back. Money players aren't that hard to find. If there isn't money in a game, don't waste your time. Don't even bother pissing on the fellow who plays "just for fun"—even if he's on fire.

You want long-haired sheep. They hang out where rich people hang out, like country clubs and high-end bars. That's where you need to be. Get nice clothes and (eventually) a nice car. Spend a dollar. You'll need a good haircut and you'll have to keep yourself groomed nicely. If you talk like a slug or a thug, fix that. Watch political shows on TV until you can talk like them—same accent, same words. Read the paper. Remember jokes. If you're from a good family? Great! You can skip this step. If you're not, learn to blend in. If you've got tattoos, remember that you might spend time in a country club locker room with these fairies, and they might see them. Tattoos are cool with vanillas now, so many tattoos will be fine. But if you've got any jail-house ink on you, keep some CoverBlend Corrective Leg & Body Makeup around and cover up before you head to the club. When you start winning, take a golf lesson or two. A few weeks with a pro should be enough for you to talk a passable game. Do the same with tennis. You've got to learn all the shit rich people do. Believe me, it isn't hard. Rich doesn't mean smart. Or talented. It just means rich. I'm a single-digit handicap and I'm a 3.1 at tennis. That's not really true, but knowing the lingo and how to hold a club are enough to give the impression that you're one of them. You've got to walk like a duck, talk like a duck, and hang around with ducks if you want to fuck ducks.

Once you look, act, and smell right, it's easy to go shopping for suckers. Look for them where rich people hang out—country clubs, expensive bars, etc. Don't push for games. They have to come to you. People worry about being cheated by strangers. Be a friend first and then a cheat. There are times when you have to push, but always try to wait for someone else to bring up the idea of poker. You can talk about Scrabble and Rummy, but let someone else say the magic word first. Make them work you.

It was a lot harder when I started out. I really had to sniff around. In those days, broads and gays never talked poker, it was only a man's game. Movie stars play on TV now, and everyone wants to do it. You should know when poker is showing on television (which is now almost twenty-four hours a day). Know which channels. Just go into a fancy-ass bar, tip the barkeep to turn on poker, and keep your eyes and ears open. Listen to who's interested. Listen to who pretends they know the game. This is your new friend. You'll be buying this guy a drink. Fuck, cheats have it easy these days. Thank you, Jesus.

Once poker comes up, talk big about your own poker play. Bring up the time you sat at a table in Atlantic City with one of the guys on TV (just pick one whose name you can remember) and talk about how you took sixty bucks off of him after he folded to you on a great bluff. Nothing too impressive. People who believe they're good poker players are trying to find you. They're looking for games. Every man believes he's better than average at poker. Maybe you'll meet some who are. Who the fuck cares? Maybe you'll meet the best in the world. You'll be cheating and you'll win.

You want confident, aggressive opponents with money. The ones who are good players won't mind when you hand them a bad beat because they know it's part of the game. Just don't let your math get too out of whack—good players will notice you making too many gut-shot straights in one night. Don't worry too much; they know people get lucky and you're going to be very lucky—for a few weeks, anyway—and then you'll be gone. Mr. Bigshot will have a few stories. He'll get his money's worth.

It doesn't take too much math or common sense to know that you'll hit mostly average players. There are a lot below average, too. The below-average players have to be strung along. You'll have to build them up to make your money. If they're playing stupid and praying for a flush, answer their prayers a few times. You are god. You control their poker universe. They win when you want them to win and they lose when there's the most money on the table. If you're not burning a game, if you think there's enough money there for next week, it's never a bad idea to dump a small pot on the last hand. They'll remember that good feeling for weeks.

I used to plant an old deck wherever I was looking for games, to help push the talk toward poker. But all that's changed. Poker always seems to come up. That's not the problem anymore; the problem now is finding the real money games. A lot of nerds really do play cards for the game of it, for fun. They play for "bragging rights." Can you buy a new car with bragging rights? Have hookers started taking bragging rights? Those people waste your time and give you nothing. So, sniff out the money. Find the guys who are betting on golf. Guys who bet, bet on everything.

You can try looking for action at the pool hall. It isn't as rich as a country club, but at least there's money around and it's filled with guys who aren't afraid to gamble. If you ask around, maybe someone will ask you what stakes you like. That's a good sign. You can make your nut on guys who want any kind of action; you might get approached to play pool for money, but if you shy away from that and the subject of cards comes up, you'll likely find yourself a real game.

Things are going crazy. Poker is even taught at community college—but if those people had money, would they go to community college? Sometimes retirees take classes, or people who want to get ready for a big trip to a casino. Get into college courses on gambling if you can find them; everyone there will want to play. And if they're willing to pay for a lecture, I'm sure they'll be grateful to you for the lesson you'll give them on hard knocks. This is a last resort; there's no big money, but at least you'll get gas money.

The Internet is a great way to find players. This technology lets you bring together people from all over the world and fleece them. There are Web sites and bulletin boards where people with similar interests write back and forth. Look for people looking for poker games. Just be careful: The Internet can also attract law enforcement professionals.

Which brings up an interesting fact: law enforcement professionals *love* poker. They love poker more than any other group, except for maybe the gang at Gambler's Anonymous. (Don't knock it; I've found a huge number of big-money games there with people who can't quit. If they haven't got the willpower, fuck them.) It's never a bad idea to have a law enforcement professional at your home game. It's almost always illegal to run a home game, but the cops don't care. With the law right there in the room, it's automatically "okay." If there's any trouble, Officer Fife will "handle it." It's a beautiful thing; law enforcement professionals can lose their jobs for taking part in home games, and sometimes reminding them of that fact can take care of any problems that come up. Honest flatfoots don't have any money, but the straight ones are less likely to play poker. In my experience, all law enforcement professionals are crooked.

You'll find what works for you. Don't limit yourself. Think about who you want to play with, who you're most comfortable becoming quick friends with. If you're good with superficial wealthy people, hit the country clubs. If you're young and like the frat boy scene, stick around colleges and take Mom and Dad's money from the kids. If you can relate to the guys on a construction crew, you'll always find a game; you'll just need to play more often to make it worthwhile. That's okay, you can do that. Best is if you can play in all these games. Wear jeans and whistle at girls when you have to; put on a suit and talk about stocks if that's the scene. The more games you're in, the more money you'll make. Be yourself. Just be the self that gets people to put money on the table with you.

Chapter 10

MAKING IT MORE INTERESTING

Home games are fun. Friends are trying to fuck friends. When you sit at the table you'll never show it, but you're there on business. You're not hoping to win money for nothing; you're planning to earn money by cheating. Everyone needs to believe you're having the most fun at the table (when you seem to have fun, they have fun). You may enjoy your work, but you're not there to have fun. You're working until you get home to count your money. Then you can really whoop it up.

People who play home games for pleasure waste a lot of time. The pace of play in a casino is much faster. The more hands, the faster the casino rake adds up. If everyone lost their money in twenty minutes instead of five hours, the casino would make a lot more per hour. You're limited by the speed of the home game. You aren't going to play six home games in a night—once you're at a game, you're committed for the evening. Be prepared to have people playing slow and telling stories; that's what you have to do to fit in and keep everyone happy about losing their money.

Make it work to your advantage. Be a good listener and tell good tall tales and make slightly funny jokes. You'll be playing cards and chatting at the same time; the people you play against will make mistakes while they're trying to figure out why Moses and Jesus were playing golf in the first place.

You'll spend some time with a bunch of guys who really don't care about the money. These guys play games like Limit Hold 'Em. Don't waste your time with low-limit games because they're never worth it. Try to change Limit Hold 'Em to No Limit Hold 'Em. Start right away. If they won't make the change, you need to get out of the game. Limit Hold 'Em is completely different from No Limit Hold 'Em, but they won't know that, and it usually doesn't take too much of a push to get them to make the switch. No Limit is sexier.

People like Limit Hold 'Em because it's cheap to see the flops, turns, and rivers. You can almost never bet anyone out of a pot, so you wind up with a table of nine guys going all the way to fifth street on nearly every hand, hoping for a miracle. In poker, cheats can make miracles happen, but in Limit, they happen all the time even without cheating. Because there are so many players, the pots do get fairly big, but at five- and ten-cent games, you can work all night for a couple of hundred bucks. Why bother? It's not worth getting up in the afternoon.

You're not going to convince anyone to play poker. They need to convince you to play poker. Even if you have to twist their arm, it has to be their idea. You can't let them see you as a hustler. But once you're in a game, suggesting that you bump the stakes a little is a fine thing to do. Get yourself on a losing streak and then push them to give you a chance to "get even." Once you get the limits up, start steering them toward No Limit.

You might not want to push too hard the first time you sit down with limit players. Feel them out, check out their bankrolls. And, obviously, I'm not just talking about how many chips they buy. See what they're driving. See what they're wearing. See what jewelry they have. Don't just look at it, see it.

People can always lose more money than they plan to in home games. You want players who have enough money so they can lose big. You don't want to get in the business of collecting debts. You want people to have the money you're going to take from them. The worst, most pathetic loser gambler won't be able to get too deeply into a home game on just his credit. His friends will cut him off before you even get there. It's very rare that people will lose it all-in a home game. No matter how much you take people for, they'll always have money left—nobody bets the farm in home games, not even farmers.

People play with others who are at about the same level in terms of budget. A good country club game should see each player ready to lose about $15K, and to be back again in another couple of weeks, ready and eager to do it again. A blue-collar game should be good for between a hundred and four hundred dollars. It'll piss them off to lose it, and it'll hurt them when they lose, but if they couldn't afford it, they wouldn't be playing.

In home games, the winner usually rotates. The players are all at about the same skill level and they get used to feeling that the luck moves around. Bob wins $500 one week, Frank might win it the next week, Hank the week after that, round and round. It's just good fun, and a guy who's too much better than everyone else week after week doesn't get invited back. The same money gets passed around the group. You need to run that weekly $500 up to $1,500, and burn the last game for about five grand before splitting town. If you can do that to four games a month, you'll be making good money.

Ask questions to get them thinking about bigger stakes. "Hey, any of you guys ever played No Limit?" That'll start the stories. Some will exaggerate; others will flat out lie to your face (imagine, people doing that!). Suggest that maybe one week they should give it a try, "just for fun." In a nine-player game, each player's chances of winning it all are one in nine. If that were true, it would be pretty good odds. Your chances of winning are much higher.

One in nine (or one in however many players you have) is great—it's a big return on the money. If someone loses, they get another chance the next week. Most players believe that they're one of the better players at the table, so they'll think their odds are even better. The probability of anyone other than you winning is zero, but they'll think their odds against the field are pretty good. The ones who know they're horrible players will hope to get lucky. You can push the conversation around that way while letting them do most of the talking. You're going to win, but they don't know that yet. You'll give them hope, and they'll love you for it. You're helping make their lives richer and more worthwhile.

Guys thank me all the time after I've cleaned everyone out. Broke and busted players tell me they've learned a lot about poker and about life from watching me. Who am I to say they haven't learned anything? I don't know—maybe there's a lot to learn by being cheated. They beg me to play again. Suckers think that their time will come to swoop in and clean up. If they read this book, maybe it will.

If, after a couple of weeks, you can't get a game to switch to No Limit, just cash out early and go home. Give off a vibe of being bored. Not a bad loser—just that you find the limit game to be dull. Tell them it doesn't get your heart pumping. Make a few jokes, thank everyone, but be dismissive of the game. Home games don't like to lose players, and you're the life of the party. A good host will volunteer to have a No Limit game just to keep you around. Take as much money as you can that night, and burn the game forever. You won't get them to play No Limit again. If it's that hard to turn them, you're not going to make a lot, so you should leave with something for your few weeks of work.

Hosts sometimes avoid No Limit because busted players get bored sitting in the corner when they get knocked out, and leave early. You'll keep them in the game as long as you can, but some people have to get cleaned out so you can get to the others. Find things for the eliminated players to do after they're eliminated. Put a game on the TV. Have the losers square off for a "loser's pot." Get two games going. You sometimes have to keep the losers happy to keep the future losers playing. It's not really that hard; the winners will want to keep playing. If you're burning a game, fuck the losers. If there are a few more weeks in the game, you'll have to keep the losers happy.

Limit games are often more trouble than they're worth, but they can be plums. People who only play limit games get used to the idea of calling every raise and playing any two cards. For a straight player, that's a scary thought . . . but since you'll always have the best cards when you need them, these games can be quick and profitable. All you have to do is get the stakes up to a decent amount and bleed enough from the game week after week.

Chapter 11

WORKING YOUR FRIENDS

I play in most games for a few months and then split. There are a few big-money games that I can keep sucking money out of, and they are worth traveling for—like the game in Charleston that I keep going back to. I cleaned them out for several weeks straight, and they all latched on to the idea that I'm some kind of great undiscovered pro player. That changed things. Now, they *want* me to beat them. I guess this is the scam the professional poker players are working now. You'll never run out of people who'll line up to lose money to a really good player. I've learned a bit about human nature in my line of work, but suckers seeking out people who can take their money—that's still a mystery to me. The Charleston guys want me to beat them and then give them some tips. I tell them colorful stories and use folksy language. I can't tell them any of my really good stories, so I make shit up.

They don't know I'm a cheater; they think I'm a rounder. Most of them have never left the Carolinas; they like the romance of a guy playing cards for a living, getting by on his skill. It would break their little motherloving hearts to know I'm a guy who cheats for a living, getting by on guile.

They're good guys. They're almost friends, I guess. I still cheat every time we sit at the table, but I don't want to burn the game even though the money isn't that great. They fawn all over me. They treat me really well. They listen to every word I say. I give them poker advice, and every once in a while I'll tell them something stupid just to see if they'll do it . . . and they always do. I told them that 10–2 was a great starting hand in Hold 'Em. Doyle Brunson won two *World Series of Poker* championships in a row with that hand. That's true, but it's not a good hand. All six of them will play that hand every time they're dealt it now. I dealt it to three of them at once, put rags on the table, and won the pot with my jack-high. I said these guys were nice; I never said they were smart.

Don't get lulled into thinking the guys you play with are your friends. You're their friend, but they're not yours. They're sacks of cash with faces. Once in a while, you'll meet some that you'll actually like. Don't go soft. You can't fuck them right if you go soft. If you don't want to fuck everyone every chance you get, get out of the game. You might start saying or doing things you shouldn't. They all trust you, always; you never trust them, ever.

Living a secret life is exciting and sexy. You'll like it, but it can get difficult once in a while. You can't talk about it with anyone. No one. People like to bullshit and brag and you can't, not for real. You'll make up shit to brag about at the tables, but it's not the real shit. A lot of grifters get into working in teams just because they can't stand not having someone to talk to. They give up 50 percent of the take because they can't keep their yaps closed. They want to brag, they want to gossip, they want to compare notes. These are the same guys who like to get caught. Then they can brag to their parole officers.

Never boast about your cheating to anyone. Not a stranger on a bus, not to a hooker in a motel room. You do what you do, and part of what you do is shutting the fuck up about what you do. Talking about cheating won't get you laid. People don't get how hard it is. They want to hear sexy stories about it, and then they think a little more about it and decide that you're a scumbag; you took candy from a baby. They can't understand how hard you work, or how important you are to the people you fuck. They don't see how every bad beat you hand out is a story you tell with cards. They don't even see it as your job. However much they want to hear the stories, however clever and sexy it seems to them while you're talking . . . after they think about it, they'll treat you like some kind of loser. If they could understand, they'd be doing it. If you understand, you'll keep your mouth shut. There's not much to brag about anyway; you didn't cure cancer, so what's to be so proud about? Tell one whore and she'll end up thinking you're an asshole, and then you'll get busted and fucked up. Trust me on this one: Shut up.

Remember that your friendship has to be one-sided. It's a divided highway. If you really need a friend, find someone completely outside of poker. Even then, never talk about what you do for a living. Don't let him know you even play cards. There can never be any overlap between your chums and your chumps.

These guys in Charleston were always in awe of me. Normally, I don't want anyone thinking I'm a pro because it cuts into my money. If I'm lucky one week, the other players might get lucky the next week—who knows? (*I* know—they won't.) The Charleston guys think I'm a pro and I still get money off of them. I told Flash in the Charleston game that I would sometimes get paid $2,000 a night for personal lessons. Flash had another group of guys he played with, and after our game he pulled me aside and asked if I'd come in and beat them all—just for fun.

I agreed. I'm mighty agreeable when it comes to taking other people's money. I made the deal with Flash that he'd secretly stake me $200 and I'd give him 50 percent of the winnings. Before the new game, I chatted with a pug called Stumpy, one of the new players. We had a private little talk and I confided in him that I was in

Flash's weekly game and I was always the winner. I let slip the fact that Flash really wanted me to clean everyone out. Without much work, I made a secret deal with Stumpy that he'd stake me $200 and I'd give him 50 percent of my winnings.

This is called *cross-staking:* Two guys stake me for 50 percent of the winnings, but they don't know about each other. Now, you may wonder what happened to the winnings. I promised 50 percent to two people, that doesn't leave much for me. Here's what I did: I played $200 and flushed all of it. I cheated to lose. I took a nice little bath with other people's money.

After the game, I was still up $200. That's not enough to bend over and pick up off the ground, but I had that game primed for the next time. I offered Flash and Stumpy each the chance to stake me again, and they both politely passed. When I won the freeze-out that next game, I took home a few grand. Flash and Stumpy both kicked themselves for not staking me that time. Perfect.

Being buddies sometimes means putting in some effort. Usually, you only have to do that work to get invited into a game. Maybe a pigeon you're setting up has kids, so you offer to pick them up from school when his car is in the shop. Maybe you lend a hand when your friend is stuck in the parking lot and you stop to help fix his flat tire. He'll be grateful and want to hang with you some day, and maybe you'll wind up playing cards. He'll never know you let the air out of his tires in the first place. You made him feel good about you, letting him know you cared enough to help. A guy you want to play cards with loses his dog, you're the guy that brings little Scruffy back to him. He'll never know you nabbed the mutt in the first place, and it'll make him feel great to have his best friend back. He'll feel better about all the people in the world. It's not a bad part of your job.

You want the people in your regular games to owe you. You want a lot of trust when you're going to be cheating. Build all the trust you can. Borrow money one week and pay it back the next week. Pay all your loans back quickly, and your friends won't worry that you're a degenerate gambler. They'll just think you're an honest guy trying to make ends meet. Don't try this in the big-money games, of course. Rich people have to know you're rich—just like them. But in your hardworking lower-class games, it'll really help. With trust, you can borrow money one week and offer to play for the debt the week after, "just to make it interesting." Sometimes you'll win and sometimes you'll lose (your choice, not theirs), and it gets a little extra money in play. You can squeeze more out of generous people. If they lose the bet for your debt, they won't feel bad about it because you need the cash. It's a way for nice people to give you a little charity when you're too proud to take handouts. You won it "fair and square," and they can feel good about losing that money.

When you're ready to burn a game and split town, get the stakes up on one hand and offer up the pink slip for your car. Friends won't be eager to play for such high stakes, but explain that you've got three cars and the one you drove in that night has a blue-book value of, say, $5,000. Put the pink slip in the pot for $1,000 and take $4,000 back in chips. Sometimes people go for it. You'd be surprised how rarely people look closely at the pink slip. No one carries a pink slip on them, so you go to your car to get it. If you want to grab anything nice lying around their house on the way out and stash it in your car, that's fine. You're burning the game that night and will never see them again. When it's time to go, you buy back your pink slip for $1,000, even though you got $5,000 for it ($4,000 in change). If they notice, it's an honest mistake. If they don't, it's four grand you don't have to cheat for. It all adds up.

I love jokes. That's one of the reasons I got into this line of work. Card players like jokes, and it pays to always have a few. They don't all have to be poker jokes, but a few that are about poker will serve you well. A few minutes after you've taken a big pot is a good time for a joke; it reminds everyone else that they're really there to have fun. Don't do groaners. Tell good jokes. Here are a couple of good jokes.

Tell this one like it happened to you. Comics sometimes start jokes like they really happened. "I was in a hardware store the other day, and the Pope and a rabbi came in . . ." Get them to believe this joke happened to you, right up until the punchline.

> *When I was out in Vegas a while ago, there was this guy standing in front of the Riv asking everyone for money. I asked him why he needed the money.*
>
> *He says to me, "My wife desperately needs an operation. I really need help."*
>
> *I was up front with him. I said, "I don't believe you. You're just going to take the money, run right back into that casino, and gamble with it."*
>
> *The guy looks at me and says, "Oh, I've got gambling money!"*

You can add your own details to it. If you tell it right, they won't know it's not a real story until the very end.

Here's another good one to learn. It has a little bad language, so you have to pick the crowd. You can't tell this one as a real story, so just start right up with it being a joke.

> *A guy worked all his life in Pittsburgh. One day he wakes up and hears a voice in his head: "Quit your job, sell your car, sell your house, go to Vegas."*
>
> *The guy figures he's been working too hard, so he ignores it and goes to his job. Every day, he hears the voice, louder and more often:*

"Quit your job, sell your car, sell your house, go to Vegas!"

This guy's been in the same job for twenty years, and he doesn't want to throw that all away. But every day, the voice comes back. He tries to ignore the voice, he goes to therapy, he gets on Prozac, but week after week, month after month, the voice just gets louder: "QUIT YOUR JOB, SELL YOUR CAR, SELL YOUR HOUSE, GO TO VEGAS!"

Finally, the poor guy can't take it anymore, so he quits his job. He puts his house up on the market and takes the first offer that will give him cash. He sells his car, and he cashes in his retirement options. He takes all the cash and he buys a ticket to Vegas.

When he steps off the plane, the voice says, "GO TO CAESARS PALACE." He hops in a cab and goes up the Strip. He enters the front doors. The voice says, "GO TO THE ROULETTE TABLE." The guy doesn't even check in. He makes his way past the slots, past the blackjack tables, and pushes his way to the first roulette wheel he sees. "PUT IT ALL ON 13-RED."

The guy takes his roll of cash, slaps it down on 13-red, and the dealer spins the wheel. The ball goes round and round, eventually slowing . . . it bounces around different numbers until it finally lands on 26-black.

The voice says, "FUCK!"

It's a good joke and it keeps the idea in the other players' heads that even if they get cleaned out, they can afford it. It's all-in fun. If you can't tell a joke, don't try. Skip it and just be a nice guy. Butchering a joke, or trying to be funny when you're not, will only hurt you as a crossroader. You want people to like you so they'll have a great time, even when they're handing you all their cash.

◦ Chapter 12 ◦

MATH: 1 IN 1 IS BETTER THAN 1 IN 2, OR 10 TO 1

S adly, cheating isn't all just smiling, charming, and finger-flinging—you have to know a little math to make money. I never cared enough about school to cheat on exams, and the only lesson I walked away with was that school turns out people who think they're smarter than they are. Even so, to be successful as a cheat, you have to understand some of the math.

You don't have to be Albert Einstein, but you're dealing with money and probability and time spent and money earned. That's math, and knowing a little math makes your winning look more like skill. If you can't do math, you won't know if you're winning or losing in the long run. You need to understand that if you're going to be making the most money you can be making.

If you don't know your basic multiplication tables, learn them. It's only memorization. Be able to do basic arithmetic in your head. You have to know a thing or two about probability, too, because if you win too many 175-to-1 shots, it'll look a bit fishy to the fish. Buy a real poker book to learn some of that shit, but don't waste too much time. Just get a feel for it.

Here's a good way to think about odds: If your odds are not 100 percent, you haven't learned anything from this book. But, for the little math you'll need, just forget big numbers. They don't exist. Forget tiny numbers, they don't exist either. You don't give a fuck about galaxies or molecules, you care about money and you never care about the pennies. A guy who can figure chances down to .00001 can still lose. It takes extra time to be that accurate, and it's not any more useful to you. Round off. Round off everything except your winnings. The difference between 26.2451 percent and 22.89453 percent is . . . none. They're the same; they're both one in four.

Think this way about big numbers: If something happens one out of two times, then it's happening to you right now. If it happens one out of ten times, it'll happen tonight. One out of a hundred won't happen tonight, but you'll see it this year. One out of a thousand might happen once in your life. Above that is bullshit. You might know someone who experiences something that's a one in ten-thousand chance; one in 100,000 is something you might hear about on the news, and one in a million or above happens to some asshole in China and gets on CNN.

You think that's dumb? Sure, million-to-one long shots happen every day. There are millions of people in the world, so there must be thousands of million-to-one events that will happen by this time tomorrow. But they won't happen to you. And if they don't happen to you, you don't really give a tinker's damn now, do you?

Losers tend to get stuck on the idea that if something might possibly happen, then it probably will. Maybe they'll get lucky. Maybe their lottery numbers will hit. They won't. But what about that hayseed who won ten million bucks in Atlantic City on his birthday? It happened. But it didn't happen to you. It happened to a loser. It won't happen to you and I'll give you a hundred to one it won't.

This is why you're reading a book about cheating. The chances that I'll win money at a game of poker are one in one. Those are acceptable odds. You want to win like me and that's why you're reading this book. Gambling is for fools, and you'll be using that fact to your advantage. People believe in luck and streaks and getting impossible cards. That's great for the card cheat. When someone bets the farm (literally), and you get that one lone card in the deck that can save your ass, they won't look at you with suspicion. They'll be mad, sure, but they'll think it's luck—either their own bad luck or your dumb luck. Don't waste your time believing in luck. Losers are lucky—cheaters go to work.

Don't allow yourself to get sucked into thinking that unlikely events might happen. I've heard many guys I take money from say that you're more likely to get hit by lightning than you are to win the lottery. They claim that they know they'll never win outside bets like those, but deep down they believe "if you don't play, you can't win." It's true, but it's a terrible bet. If your odds of winning a million dollars are a million to one and you play every day, you won't win in your lifetime. That's really drawing dead.

If you realize the odds of winning are the same as getting hit by lightning, but you keep playing the lottery anyway, you're just wasting my money until I meet you. Do you live your life thinking that getting hit by lightning is a possibility? You may not go dancing in the rain while wearing metal underwear on the golf course, but you don't hide under your bed when you hear thunder, do you? You know that risk is out there, but it's tiny. It's so tiny that you don't even think about it.

The point is, don't try to live your life or make your decisions based on things that are wildly unlikely. If it's greater than a one in a thousand chance, don't think about it. Don't worry about it and don't gamble on it. One in one is the only odds I take.

If you're figuring out odds in the game while you're waiting to cheat, you want to get close enough to be practical. When you're sitting at a card table, three-thousandths of a percentage point has no impact on your decision. Neither does one percentage point.

You want to figure those numbers fast. This isn't Harvard, you won't get extra credit for being exact.

You won't have a calculator at the table. You can memorize the probabilities for hitting draws that will improve your hand, or for how many times a certain hand will win against a set number of players, and that information will be more than you'll really need. You can get away with a good feel for the game, and an understanding of how often something will or won't happen for you, but you always need to think about your poker game in terms of money. At times you'll put in extra hours or dump some hands in order to make more money. You want to get primed for a bigger take, so you buy beer for eight guys and throw them $300 one week; you should know how much you need to win the next week to make it worthwhile.

Time and effort aren't free. You should always get paid well for what you do. If it takes you a day of travel and eight hours of play to win $500, you should know what your expenses are and figure out how much you're pulling in per hour.

If a guy you're playing with will bet $50 into a $5,000 pot, you know that he doesn't understand pot odds, and you can use that. If another guy bets hundreds of dollars on a hand that has less than a 2 percent chance of improving, you can use that, too.

It's good to know the odds, it will make your game seem real and believable. But keep in mind . . . the chances of your winning any game must always be 100 percent.

Chapter 13

MAKING YOUR MARKS

Everyone knows about marked cards. Marking is a tool that's been around as long as cards have been around—probably even longer. When Hollywood know-nothings make movies about cheats, they feature marked cards. Read anything about cards and gambling and you'll see something about marked cards.

Since everyone knows marked cards exist, people think they're safe. They think that just knowing something exists protects them against it. Try that with tigers. I know bacteria exist, but I still wash my hands after playing patty-cake with a hobo. You can use marked cards *because* everyone knows about them, and no one knows anything about them.

You mark a deck so that you can tell what's on the front of a card by looking at the back of the card. This is a good example of cheating. If you were supposed to be able to tell the value of a card by looking at the back, we would all be playing with cards that have the value printed on both sides. For all practical purposes, you will be.

There are many ways to do it, but the end result is always the same. The mechanics are different, but the gist is that you'll know what other people are holding with a quick glance. You don't control which cards they're holding like you can with fancy dealing or hold-out methods, but knowing which cards the other players have is more than enough for you to win. Some markings are really only useful when you're the dealer, unless you have great eyesight.

All marking systems are easy. You'll want to try them all and learn them all. Find the best fit for your normal working conditions. You want to get your work down using your host's cards, rather than swapping in your own *readers*. Marking someone else's cards on the fly at the game is better. Then you don't have to worry about anyone noticing a difference in the decks. A lot of the time, used decks are honest readers that have been marked for you with coffee stains, small rips, scratches, and so on. If you bring in your own deck, and it doesn't have the exact same level of wear and stickiness, people will notice.

Here's a cute little trick with marked cards that they sell at magic stores. It lets you read the value of any card in the deck from the other side of the goddamned room. The name of the card is written in big bold red letters on the back of a standard red deck. The red inks for the writing and the back design are slightly different, but it blends in almost perfectly. Looking at any one card, you can't really tell there's writing on the back, but if you look at the cards through a red piece of cellophane (which blocks out the red on the background), there are giant letters for value and suit: "8S" for eight of spades, thick and four inches high. It's perfect if you have red cellophane built into your eyes. The magic store sold the deck along with a clipboard that had red cellophane in a window. What kind of idiot would use a thing like that?

I knew just the guy.

I found a small game with a bunch of dairy people (never play with farmers); they had plenty of money and nice homes, but they still drove old pickups and they never could be pushed into serious money games. It was that frugal Midwest thing. I buddied up with all of them and sat in on their game once a month, even though it wasn't worth the drive. I guess I liked ripping off subsidized farmers. They were playing with your tax money.

Junior, the most trusting of the bunch, had told me that Ploppy—a two-faced old coot—had complained to all the other guys in that game that I was cheating. I *was* cheating, of course, but he didn't know it. I get pissed at being slandered about something no one really knows I'm doing. Get it right, or shut the fuck up. I hadn't taken more than a couple hundred bucks, barely enough to pay for the gas, and definitely not more than they could afford. Ploppy had no idea that anyone had really been cheated; he was just talking shit, and I hate that.

If you play cards for money, you'll run into a guy like Ploppy once in a while. He's a guy who thinks he's on top of the game, and if he loses, he'll be convinced that someone was cheating. He'll bitch about it to his friends, whether it was a legitimate bad beat or he simply got outplayed. The bad news is, once an asshole says that someone is cheating, the game is busted for you forever, and you have to move on without getting all your money. It's the worst way to lose a game.

Ploppy had told Junior and the others that I'd been using readers because there was no other way I could've beaten him. The truth was, I didn't have marked cards and I did little more than some glimpsing and poking the pot once in a while. I was still in the honeymoon stage, drawing them in, trying to get them to raise the stakes. I'm not going to bother marking a deck for a few hundred bucks. It didn't matter that he had no idea what was happening; he was a sore loser and he spread some venom about me using marked cards, so I had no intention of ever going back.

That is, until I saw those really crappy marked cards in the magic store.

I found a banker's visor, replaced the green plastic with clear red plastic, and made up a set of the cards. This asshole had me doing craft work, but it would be worth it. The marks were as big and as obvious as they could be. I made up two decks. I called Junior and said that I hadn't talked to him in a while because Ploppy thought I was cheating. I said I'd like to play again, and that I might want his help with a little fun surprise. I told him I'd let him in on the joke during the game.

I showed up and Ploppy was very nice to my face. Scumbag. He didn't bring up how he thought I was a cheater, and I didn't mention that I knew he'd spread lies about me (he had never caught a single thing I did). I brought in my magic store marked cards and pulled the visor low over my forehead. When you're around farmers, you can put on a funny hat and no one thinks a thing about it. I used the red cellophane as obviously as I could every time I dealt, and I won nothing but small pots.

We stretched our legs after a couple of hours and I got Junior alone. I told him I wanted him to tell Ploppy to put on the visor when he dealt; then I gave Junior my camera and asked him to take a picture of Ploppy looking stupid in the visor. I told Junior I'd use the photo for my xmas card, and Junior—like any good friend—agreed to help make another good friend look foolish.

I had in my head a few ways it could play out. The most likely was that Ploppy would see the markings and bust me out to the group; the proof of my marked cards would be sitting in the palm of his hand. Junior and I would laugh, and we'd tell him he'd been stung for talking shit about me. I'd show everyone the marked cards and the visor, the hicks would get a good laugh, and we'd play another hand. Ploppy would be mad, he'd bet a big hand to get back at me, and I'd take him for a few hundred more just to teach him a real lesson, and then I'd leave the game for good. I would cheat by nail-nicking Ploppy's own cards during play, out of a sense of poetic justice.

But that's not what happened. I got lucky (sometimes it happens even without cheating). When I told Junior about the photo, I casually mentioned that it was Ploppy who had bought me the stupid visor as a gift, which is why I wanted the photo of him wearing it. When we sat down at the table again, Junior followed my plan and Ploppy obliged. Why the fuck not? Junior even suggested that Ploppy pull the visor low on his forehead for a better picture. Right at that moment, Ploppy glimpsed the big fat markings on the cards on the table. He looked around, glared at me, and I looked around nervously. I gave him my "I'm bluffing" look and Ploppy was mine: hook, line, and sinker. He was on to me, and I couldn't have been happier.

Ploppy held on to the visor and dealt the cards. He was going to use my own readers against me. Darn it all. Too clever, that Ploppy. What an idiot; I guess he figured I'd forgotten that the visor gave the wearer super-cheater powers. Farmers. He played a hand, bet big, and took six dollars from me. He passed the cards to the next player to deal, but he held on to the visor.

"You don't mind if I keep it, do you, *friend*?" he asked. Oh my. He got me. What could I do? I couldn't admit to cheating. All the power was in his hands. I shook my head sheepishly and kept dumping hands until the deal came around to Ploppy again.

The man who was so shocked about *my* using marked cards (even though I wasn't at the time) had no trouble winning the next several hands himself using marked cards. Morality looks different through rose-colored visors.

He got the deal again, but I cut the cards for him. It wasn't my turn to cut, but I cheat for a living and I didn't find it hard to make it so no one noticed—not even Ploppy. He was too focused on taking my money with my own sneaky props. I swapped out the first marked deck with my second marked deck. And that deck was marked and stacked in a way to get him to bet a lot of money.

Before the hand was dealt, I told the table it was getting late and I had to go. No one wanted me to leave, least of all Ploppy. I eventually agreed to stay for one more hand, but then I had to run.

Ploppy dealt. He had an ace and king of diamonds. He noticed through his visor that I had a jack of spades and a jack of clubs. I made a bet, he raised me, I thought a while and called. The flop brought the four and seven of diamonds, and the king of spades. He had high pair and a flush draw. I bet big and was called. The turn was the queen of diamonds—he hit his diamond flush. I made another large bet after some hard thinking and everyone folded to ploppy. He called. The river was a seven of clubs.

I made a big bet and Ploppy raised me all-in. I thought long and hard and said, "Well, it's the last hand of the evening, what the heck," and then I went all-in, too.

Ploppy proudly showed his ace-high flush. I yelled and jumped up from the table, flipping over my queen and seven of spades: Full house . . . he lost. What a shame. I guess I must have mis-marked my queen and my seven as a pair of jacks. How unprofessional of me.

I had to do some work at that point, making a little diversion to keep Ploppy stunned long enough to cash out and get the hell out of there. I never spoke to any of them again, but I still have happy thoughts about Ploppy trying to convince Junior and the others that I'd cheated him. Junior would remember that I said it was Ploppy's visor, and when Ploppy showed them how those markings worked, he'd come off as the bad guy (and crazy, too).

That's assuming he even bothered to tell them. He probably decided to start using that amateur marking system himself, and we can only hope that he used it against the wrong guy in the back room of a biker bar.

The lesson: If you can't win when you're the dealer, find another game.

Chapter 14

PAPER-WORKING—"AHHH, THE SIX OF DIAMONDS"

Marked cards are sometimes referred to as papers, readers, or occasionally as cheaters. If you're going to mark cards, don't call them cheaters. Especially not during a game. If you need to be told that, get a fucking day job.

Now that I think of it, don't call them papers. Don't call them anything. They're cards. They aren't special. That's the trouble with all this slang. I know I covered this before, but it's worth repeating. The guys you'll be working won't know those terms, so you shouldn't either. Do you want to play cards with someone who knows all the inside work of card cheaters? You wanted to know the slang. Now you know, so forget it.

The first marking method is absolutely clean: a *one-way deck*. That's a deck with a back design that isn't the same if you turn a card upside down—like a photo of some stupid fucking dog on the back. If you reverse a card, you can spot it a mile away. All you have to do is get them facing the same way, with the aces reversed (or the court cards or all the spades) and you've got a way to see cards even if someone else deals. The nice thing about that system is that, after one deal, there's no evidence. Cards get turned around in the play of the hand, but they aren't disturbed by shuffles and cuts. You can only flag a few cards with a one-way deck, but it's better than not cheating at all.

I played in a game where the host wanted to use a fucking Frog deck that he said was made from "top quality card stock." It had the Eiffel Tower on the back, making it great for one-way work. The cards were really thin and had sharp corners. I gave myself a goddamn paper cut on the tip of my pinky while squeezing that deck to get a glimpse. Blood got everywhere, and I couldn't deal seconds for a week. The cards you can use for one-way work are usually shitty.

The system used most by amateurs is *blockout work*. You can fill in patterns on Bicycles with red or blue ink (depending upon the color of the backs, but I hope you knew that). Bicycle cards have an ornament in each corner that looks like a flower with eight petals around a dot. By filling in parts of those flowers, you can show both suit and value. You use the two flowers on the top of the card and repeat for the two flowers on the bottom, which mirror the top. Both dots white equals spades, both dots red equals hearts, outer dot only red equals clubs, outer dot only white equals diamonds. Then you fill in one of the sixteen petals to show value. You can tell at a glance what the card is. And so can anyone else. All they need to do is look closely at one card and they'll see it's marked. If they suspect you, they'll catch you. Don't use any system like this.

It'll be rare that you'll play in a game without marking a few cards. You'll be holding out and palming sometimes, but you'll be marking cards all the time. You need to know what's on the table when you're not dealing. Most of your marked cards will be marked right there, during the game. You need to create your own system and do *not* make it easy to remember. If it's easy to remember, it's easy to bust.

You'll be using plain old cards. Cards get used. They will get a smudge or a nick or a rip. Those are the only cosmetics you want on your cards.

Some half-smart players know how to *go to the movies:* You flip through the backs and look for movement on the cards. Fair cards should all look the same because they all *are* the same. Marked cards will appear to have parts of the back jump around, like an animated flipbook. Anyone can see it during the shuffle if they're observant and know what to look for. You will always see it during the shuffle because it's your job to be observant.

Your bread and butter is the nail mark. While you're looking at your cards, you put a small nick in the edge with your fingernail. It doesn't take much, and it's hard to notice. It's the kind of thing that might happen in normal card handling, except it never does. Find the minimum mark that you can spot. It won't take much—they're easier to see than you might think. Practice feeling them when you're dealing, too. When you're dealing you'll have other tools, but you'll still want your marks. You're going to spend a lot of time practicing this. Get a deck and nail-mark it. Be able to glance at the mark and feel it when it goes by in your hands. Nail-marking is what matters. Practice it, it's your life. I'm telling you, if you opened this book and all it said was "mark the fucking cards with your fingernail" you would have gotten more than your money's worth. You can build a career on that.

Create your own system. Marking patterns is for weekend cheats. It has to be your own shit and you have to know it. There's no room for thinking. You don't want to think at all. You don't want to glance at a card and say to yourself, "That nick is about halfway down on the long side and a quarter across the top, let's see, that's the ... ace of diamonds." You can't take that long to think. You can't stare at the back of the card for that long. In that amount of time, someone can see what you're doing *and* get out a knife.

You want to glance at the nick and instantly *see* the face of the card in your mind. Each nick has a memory and a story for me. I love my nicks. My card marks are the story of my life.

When I was eleven years old, a few of the older kids were teaching the rest of the kids in the neighborhood how to play poker. We did it for fun, but after a while we started playing for "real money" (real money for an eleven-year-old). I wasn't a rich kid and didn't have money for the game, but I wanted to play. I got the idea that they should let me play for "services." I bet my time and—more important to teenage boys—my obedience. For each ten cents they'd give me to play in the game, I'd be their little servant. I'd do anything they needed, for five minutes.

I lost a lot, and the winners would make me shine their bikes, do their paper routes, or steal something from the store for them. I paid my debts. We weren't goody-goodies—they never made me do their homework (none of us did homework). But I'd have to find the grownup to buy beer for us. I really hated being an errand boy, but I wanted to be with the guys, so I kept selling my time.

There was one kid I looked up to. He was fifteen and tall, and he was a good poker player. One day he gave me a really bad beat and I wound up owing him a full hour of "service." He waited a few days and then told me it was time to pay up. His mom wasn't home and he said I had to come to his room with him for an hour. You know what happened next. It didn't take a full hour, but I had to help him polish his knob. I jerked him off. After that, I still owed him forty-five minutes, which he cashed in by telling me I couldn't tell anyone, ever. Back then I didn't want anyone to know, but now . . . fuck him.

I hate losing. Whenever I think about losing at poker, I think about paying off that debt. I swore right then, I'd never lose again.

And there was one way to keep that promise to myself. That's when I figured it out. I showed up at the next game. He didn't think I would, but I did. The queerbait gave me a wink, but it didn't bother me.

The first hand dealt, I marked the ace of hearts with a nick on two of the corners. Those nicks were probably as big as the Grand Canyon compared to the work I do nowadays. I had never heard of nail nicks, it just came to me naturally. I didn't even know how much it would help, but it felt right. As soon as I marked that one card, I was scared to death. I thought everyone would see it and bust me, and I knew sissy-boy could think of some other perverted punishment for me. But no one saw it. I could see that ace from across the room. I followed that card from hand to hand. Every time I saw that little nick, I saw a big red heart floating above the card.

I felt the power. I had a knack. I knew I could win with that one small extra piece of information. That one card nick turned my "luck" around. I started winning for the first time.

That one card taught me restraint. I didn't get greedy. I was careful. The ace of hearts taught me the timing to reel them in. That ace taught me everything I know.

I didn't understand anything about playing poker "fair" (making an eleven-year-old give you handjobs is fair?), but with my little advantage, I learned everything. If I'd nicked all the aces off the bat, I would have won too much, too fast and that would've queered my chances. I didn't win every hand, but I saw that you can win more than you're supposed to and no one would notice. I saw that you don't have to win it all to come out ahead. I learned that losing a little keeps people coming back to let you win more.

I won back all of my slave markers, and then I started winning money. None of the kids had much to win, but I always came out ahead. I sure as hell made a point of taking all the gay bully's money. He was wishing I'd take a couple "I'll do anything" markers as payment, but I don't play for that team. I told him to come back when he had more real money. He did, and I took that, too. These were my greatest wins. Junkies chase their first high but never get it. Every time I nick an ace, I get to feel my first win.

I'm never going to forget the ace of hearts. I might have ended up a hardworking asshole, but because of that card, I cheat for a living. I built up my whole system like that. At first I was afraid to mark too many cards; I thought I'd get caught. I nicked my power card; then I added the king of diamonds, the queen of hearts, and the jack of spades. That's all I did for a long time. That's enough. You'll win slowly, but you'll win. It took a few weeks, but those cards got me my money. If you looked at those cards in any deck I've handled, you wouldn't see anything. It's a regular deck of cards with a little wear, a few accidental nicks here and there. You might not even be able to tell my ace from the queen of spades by looking at the backs. But I can. Always. From across the room . . . in the dark . . . on a galloping horse.

I got laid (by a woman, thanks for asking) six months later. I asked her what her favorite card was and she told me: the six of diamonds. I have a nick for that and every other card. If the six of diamonds from a strange deck touches my hand once, it's got my marking in less than a second. Once I've handled a deck of cards, they have my whole life in them. I remember each marking for the money it brought me. Does it help to know where the six of diamonds is? You bet your ass. It helps to know where any card is, and I like the memory of that woman popping into my head. The ace of hearts doesn't bring up memories of that guy; it just reminds me of how it felt when I started to win. All my markings are good memories.

Let your marking system build up nice and slowly, and have each mark mean something to you. This is going to be your life; if you do it right, you can have the table swirling with information and stories that no one else can see. You won't have to try to remember. It's a part of you. That's how you win. Don't worry about marking every card. Try to get your paint and aces first. Don't think about suit and value, think the whole card. I don't divide the top of the card into four sections for spades/hearts/clubs/diamonds and the left side into fifths for ten/jack/queen/king/ace—I don't do any of that shit. You're only talking to yourself, so you don't need a code, all you need are memories. One of my jacks and one of my aces have two marks each. I like it that way. It'll take you a while to get your marks in, but you're waiting for the pots to build anyway, and most of the cheap bastards will use the same cards week after week. I've gone back to a game after being gone a year and a half, and on my first deal I felt my sweet little six slide under my finger. There are a lot of reasons to smile.

Don't *ever* do work you don't have to do (that's against my code in every way). There may be accidental marks on the cards already. Don't nail-mark a card that has anything you can notice already on it.

Daub is another marking style. Put a little smudge on a card in a certain place. It can be red ink or anything else you can imagine. Even bleach and water will work. You might like it better than a nick because it can be easier to see, but you can't feel it. You should have your own system for daub marks, too, and don't make them the same as the nicks. You could stash a red ink pad in your lap to do fancy marking designs, but why would you? If things get hot, do you really want hard evidence sitting in your lap? Don't keep a bloody knife in your jacket pocket.

Don't use something too tacky, or cards will stick together; you don't want the deck to be thrown away. You also don't want the daub to transfer from the back of one card to the front of the card on top of it. A smudge on the front of a card is much more noticeable and harder to explain away.

Use your environment. If there's a newspaper lying around (and there always is), have a look at the box scores and plant your thumb over an inky ad. It doesn't matter if it's black. It's just a little dirt, and it will go unnoticed. Don't put blackface on the card like Al Jolson, just a little smudge so you can find it later. If there are smokers in the game, get a little ash on the tip of your pinky and use that. Black coffee works too, and so does whiskey. All you need is a little change of color. And remember, it's the back that you'll be marking.

Do I need to say that? If you're marking up the front of the cards, you should stick to hustling kindergarteners at Chutes and Ladders for their milk money. I can't even remember the last time I used daub. Use nail nicks and crimps.

Crimps are temporary, but they can be useful. A crimp is a bend in the card. You can crimp a card any way you like—in half (either way) or on the corners. A crimp is not a fold. You're not putting a crease in it, you're bending it a fraction of an inch. Cards will hold crimps through several shuffles. You need to practice to find how much you should bend it. Too much and it'll crease, too little and you'll lose it. I have memories for crimps, too. So will you.

Never crimp up. If the card is face down on the table, you don't want to crimp the corner up because that's easier for everyone to see (especially if you crimp the index). A great time to get your crimp is when you're bending the cards up to look at them when they're on the table. Pinch your index finger and thumb together on your cards, and slightly dog-ear the index toward you. A crimp makes a card very easy to see in the deck. If you can get a crimp in the aces, you can glance at the stub and know how deep the next ace is.

Some decks are better to mark than others. People who buy expensive poker cards will sometimes use one deck for years. They get fat and sticky and warped. Nothing you do to those cards will be noticed. They're already marked for you. I don't like honest readers; it's a little too close to fair play. Put your own work in play.

A flawed deck can give an advantage to anyone at the table, but no one else will know how to use that advantage. It takes practice to win a game with marked cards. The memorizing is easy; create a story about all the imperfections and little stains and rips in the deck. You can't use crimps on old cards—they won't hold up—but some good creases will already be there.

People who only play with shiny new decks will probably swap decks every few hands. And if they see a smudge after one game, they may throw those cards away. Nail marks still work in those games, just get your work down fast.

You can also *blister-mark* the cards with the edge of a knife or tip of a pin; instead of making anything visible, you rough up a part of the card. It doesn't take much at all for you to feel the pegging and not be able to see it. This is useful when you're dealing.

Nail marks are the way to go. But the real story is the six of diamonds. What a piece of ass.

Chapter 15

HIGH CARD BEATS A PAIR

Once in a pig's age, someone will come up to you and ask you to partner up with them. This will happen to you someday, either because people think you might be a cheater or they just think you're a good player who can help them win. If you know your ass from a spade, people will want your help.

Single-o Poker is the only way to go. There are a couple of team scams like *backlining* or cross-staking, but in those cases your "partner" is the one who you're cheating. Any time you bring in an *itemer*, you increase your chances of getting caught *and* you make less money.

I get secretly approached by players who want to cheat (but who don't have the brass to try it on their own). They come to me because they think that no one would suspect me. No shit.

People who want to work two-man scams are never direct about asking you to help. They're afraid you'll say no and then think less of them. They underplay it by saying, "It's not really cheating" or, "I'm just kidding," or both. They're never direct. Directness wouldn't work any better on me, but it would be refreshing.

"Hey, ever see *The Sting*? You know how they teamed up and taught those gangsters a lesson? Ha ha. That'd be fun, huh? You know, just for kicks . . . to do something like that? Wouldn't it? Just for shits and grins?"

My answer is to smile with a puzzled look on my face and say, "What's fun about cheating?"

We have a good laugh and never speak of it again. It's good for everybody. They've learned to take the high road, and I have something on them. It's good to have anything on anyone.

They want a partner in crime so they can tell stories over their beers. They'll eventually get caught, and they'll never make enough that it will be worth the beating they'll take. Real men don't have partners.

The hard part of the game of poker is finding the action, preparing the players, getting into the games, and getting away clean. As I've said, the cheating is the easy part. Do you think I love going to a country club and working a rich chump for a week just to find out he only plays a twenty-dollar buy-in "gentleman's game"? You think I like remembering his kids' names? It's the closest thing to work that I do. How much harder do you think it would be to get a partner into one of those games with me? The players have to trust you *and* your teammate. And why? To bring home half the profits after twice as much work?

There has been a grand total of four times in my entire life that I've sat at a table with another cheater who knew what he was doing. Three of those times were in back-room games at bars or clubs. Only once did I see a guy with any kind of chops cheating at a home game I was in; we must have both smelled the same bacon cooking. I gave him room to work and he stayed out of my way, too. I don't believe in "professional courtesy," but we both won as much as we could each get away with. After the game he stopped me at my car and complimented my second deal.

Who fucking cares what he thinks?

He suggested we team up and get into some other big-money games that he had been sniffing around. I said no and never bumped into him again.

At one point in the game, he'd said that he had work down. No one else at the table knew what that meant (he was telling me he had marked cards in play), but they might have asked around and found out. Why risk it? He should have been shot for saying that, and he probably will be some day. Would you go up to a 350-pound black linebacker and say, "Oh-gay uck-fay ourself-yay!" and hope to hell that he doesn't know pig latin?

The only real value in collusion is having someone at the table who thinks that *he's* the cheater (not the sucker), and he'll fall for anything. There are plenty of ways for teams to put other people through the ringer.

The easiest type of collusion is simply to agree with another player to split the night's take. That's it. You don't need signals or advanced plans. When your partner bets, you get out of his way. If you play in hands with him, he'll be winning his own (and your own) money. If he makes a raise, you raise again. The raise means he's got a good hand; your raise is just to get the other players' bets up higher. Many of them will fold, but for the ones that decide to call, your raise either sweetens the pot or drives them out. You have two chances to pick up the best hand in every pot.

It boils down to one person having twice the number of chips and two different positions at the table; that's a big edge. When you see this happening at your table (and it will), you'll be sitting pretty. Use the fact that you'll be raised and reraised to your advantage by putting your own raise in there, too. Since you're going to win (the team doubles their chances of winning, but that chance is zero against you), they're helping you get the pots big.

Catching one player between two raisers is called *sandwiching* or *whipsawing.* It's not against the rules, but if people find out that it's happening on purpose, they get pissed. It's good to know this. It's a good out for you when you've pulled down a nice big pot where you were a little bit too lucky. You can complain about being squeezed and how Jesus wouldn't be happy with that kind of underhanded play, and then pick up your chips and leave. They're violating the "spirit of the game," not you . . . and it's good to leave on the moral high ground, even if you're not coming back.

A team can use almost anything as a signal for when to dump and when to play soft. They can signal with the placement of their hands, stack their chips a certain way, bet specific amounts (odd amounts mean fold, even amounts mean raise), or use international signals. They can give office with eye contact. A couple of idiots once even tried to tap out Morse code in a game with me. I don't know moose cock about Morse code, but I recognized dashes and dots thumped out on the table felt. For fun, I thumped out little drum solos on the table whenever they tried that shit.

Once in a while (more than you would expect), you'll be invited to a *hot-seat* game. That's where a bunch of wannabe cardsharps get together to fleece one stranger (you). They invite a new guy to their home and work him over together. What a waste of time. Eight guys carving up one guy's beans. These games are always looking for players, so you'll be asked sooner or later. They never worry about the guy in the hot seat getting pissed because what's he going to do? He's outnumbered eight to one. If you're in a *hot-seat* game, you'll know it. That many players can't work together without showing their glee. They'll wink at each other and smile and overact.

The problem with a hot-seat game is that it's hard to make real money in one. The edge they get by communicating doesn't touch your ability to have whatever cards you need—you still have a 100 percent advantage—but they minimize their losses, so you won't get any big wins. When people get out of the way for each other, pots stay small. You'll want to dump a few hands, act frustrated, and start playing crazy. Get them to raise up a nice big pot, win it, and take off.

I partnered up with a guy in a back-room game in a bar one time. He had been railbirding for a couple of hours, and he followed me when I left the table for a piss break. He said he thought I was good—he knew I was cheating, but he didn't know how—and he wanted in. This was a game full of guys that I didn't want any trouble with—rednecks and bruisers—and I figured if I told him politely to go fuck himself, he'd tip them off. So we picked a place to settle up after the game, I gave him a signal to fold and a signal to raise, and he joined the game. He could barely keep a straight face. I doubled off; for a while, I had him winning a bunch of hands, then I started "getting lucky." In the past, the most money that game ever had on the table was ten grand and we broke the record that night. As everyone headed out, he shot me a wink.

I brought down nearly sixteen large with my partner's help. A split with my partner gave me eight grand, which is a good night's work. Splitting town with all of it would be an even better idea. So that's what I did. Maybe he shouldn't have trusted the good card cheat to divvy up the cash.

Even though you won't be partnering up, you can lay *neves* that other people will try teaming up against you. It's a beautiful thing; they'll think they're unbeatable, and then when you take them down, they'll blame each other for fucking up the system and never even dream that they've been beaten at their own game. But remember, a team of two to eight guys can beat the shit out of you better than a bunch of individuals, so don't get caught and get out fast.

Chapter 16

SHINERS

It's good to know a little something about every type of cheating device, even if you're not going to use them all. If you want to make a living by cheating at cards, you should be able to use any of the tools of the trade without getting caught. Practice and apply them until you're blue in the face and your friends are empty in the wallet.

Shiners aren't used as much nowadays—and that's good, because people have forgotten about them. A shiner is anything that will give off a reflection, like a mirror. You can't bring a mirror to a card table, but you'd be surprised by what won't get noticed. There are plenty of knickknacks that people usually keep on the table that will work fine if you put them in the right position.

The idea is this: You put your shiner on the table under the cards when you're the dealer. As you deal, you glance down and see a reflection of the indices of the cards. I use it early in the game. Deeper into the night, you're going to have your paperwork in place, the deck will be yours, and you won't need a shiner. But until then, it's nice to know the cards people have. You can learn about their play and start to figure out how you want the scene to unfold when you have full control of the table. It's also a good method if you sit down in the middle of a game and need to win fast before you can get all your nail markings down.

Focus as you deal. It's not hard, but you have to be paying attention to remember which cards you dealt to each person. The other players will forget their own cards but you'll remember every card on the table. If a player does forget what cards he has in the hole, don't remind them, let them look. It's off-pissing, but always remember that you're not supposed to know anyone else's cards.

Once you know all the down cards on the table and which cards you have, you'll be able to make very informed bets. If you think having too much information would be unfair, then play every hand without looking at your own cards.

You don't have to know everyone's cards anyway. A couple cards from a couple of players will do you fine. With a shiner, it's easy to glimpse the guy on your left; there are better angles and a built-in distraction for the guy on your left. He gets his cards first, so he'll be busy looking at them right away. The dirty work comes early, when people are waiting for their own cards. Once cards are on the table, a lot of players will watch each other, and you want to get all your dirty business done before anyone is watching you.

You're going to have to look around for the right shiner. You want something that makes perfect sense to have with you. A silver pocket watch isn't going to work. What are you doing to do, dress up like a riverboat gambler? A monocle might make for a good *gaper,* but unless you dress like a rich Kraut, it won't look natural to have one on you.

Highly polished cigarette lighters are a good choice if you're a smoker. So are cigarette cases. If a shiner works well for you, you might want to start smoking if you don't already. Smoking will give you more reasons to reach around the table for ashtrays, and a cigarette in your hand can work well to shade a palmed card. Not only that, smoking will help keep you awake, relaxed, and alert. No, smoking isn't good for you, but neither is taking money from guys who are bigger than you, and you're going to do plenty of that. You'll be able to afford the best fucking doctor in the world, and by the time you get sick from smoking, money might buy you a cure. If smoking is better for your game? Smoke. If a lighter works for you? Smoke. At least smoke while you're playing with shiners, and then quit both (good luck).

You don't need a mirror finish. The shiner will be directly below the cards as you deal, and even brushed metal can give off a good enough reflection to see what you need to see. A mirror finish looks too much like something that you put on the table to reflect the fucking cards.

A carefully placed ring can work beautifully. It helps if it has some flat spots so the image doesn't distort too much. A ring is the easiest shiner to conceal and to position. Many home players are using plastic cut cards (like the casinos do). They're supposed to stop people from seeing the bottom card during the shuffle, but they're shiny plastic, and the red and green ones can be slid forward on the bottom of the deck during your deal, and they can shine for you right there, in the perfect position. Sunglasses work well, too, and thanks to poker on television, players will wear sunglasses because they think they are getting an edge and looking cool. They'd look cooler if they were smoking.

I don't use shiners much, but when I do, I'll often keep my lighter and cigarettes in my pocket and use the other players' shit. They never figure you would use their shit for that. Just move their sunglasses or lighter "out of the way" for the deal, and there you go. If they open a door, you walk right in. They should know better.

One fat slob had me over for a home game where he offered up really crappy plastic chips to play with. They looked like they were from a kid's toy chest. My nice shiny stack of blue $1 chips made pretty reflections. If the host is too cheap to buy real chips, why not make the most of the situation?

An old-timer told me once that they call them "shiners" because if you get caught using them, you'll get socked in the eye. I've never been busted using a shiner because I don't make it obvious. I only glance; I don't stare down at it. If you miss a reflection, don't lose your dealing rhythm. Never change your dealing rhythm for anything. If you miss a glance, move on. You'll get it next time. If you plan to use shiners all the time or if you never plan to use them, practice this move until it's as easy as seeing the time on a clock. When you need it, you're going to need it to be automatic.

In the last couple of years I've moved to a new shiner. I invented this one myself and the beauty is that it draws no heat whatsoever: drinks. Dark drinks, like cola or coffee, work the best. No ice in the cola, please. No cream in the coffee, thanks (black coffee tastes good with a cigarette). The black liquid surface works beautifully. You'll have plenty of opportunity to use this because drinks are always on the table and they're at the right height and in the right position. If you're worried someone's suspicious, throw some cream or a couple of ice cubes in. The best part is, you can get your host to get you a refill—isn't that kind of him?

I've seen more than my share of *chaffers* that use shiners. The trend now is to use whatever you're protecting your cards with: little discs or toys that you put on your cards to show you're still in the hand. Why would you use something like that? "Oh, I use this coke mirror for my card protector for sentimental reasons." If you use something like that, it won't be in the right position; a card protector shouldn't be anywhere but on top of your cards. If you think you can use a real mirror—even for practice—give up now. Go practice smoking instead, you moron.

Chapter 17

DO YOU KISS YOUR MOTHER WITH THAT MOUTH?

F riends like to laugh and have fun with each other. A big part of the game for many poker players is that it's a great time to pal around. The locker room mentality takes over, and a poker game is a safe place for many men to talk about things they don't usually have a chance to get into elsewhere. It's one of the reasons some wives don't like poker. Some wives also don't like when their men lose their shopping money to a guy like me in a poker game.

Most of the things that men say are lies. They may brag about pussy or promotions or a genius play in a high-stakes game that never happened. It makes them feel good to bond with other men, and you can use that freedom to help take their money.

In just about any group of guys, someone will tell an off-color joke or story. It won't happen at the start of the night, but it'll happen once the booze starts flowing. When it does—whatever race, sex, creed, or color is joked about—you will be very offended.

Of course you don't really care. You don't give a fuck what anyone says. You don't really care about sexism, racism, or anythingism. You're there to make money. But, to make money, you should act offended. Not deeply offended, but a little bit offended. Politely offended. What happened to my advice about always being friendly and always fitting in? This is a special situation. It might work for you. If you can't be the most likeable guy at the table, this might work for you. The payback can be good.

This would never have worked when I started out, but it works great these days. When I started out, I retold every dirty and racist joke I heard and I wrote a few myself. But times have changed. Now everybody thinks about how what they say or do makes people feel. They get apologetic. Even if they aren't really sorry about a comment or a joke (and they never are), the social pressure is high to never say certain things.

You can knock your opponents for a loop. This makes them jittery and self-conscious and it puts people on edge. Then, they're more likely to make mistakes. It also makes you the Pollyanna at the table. You're the tightass. You're the goody two-shoes. A sensitive guy like you would *never* cheat. And at the end of the night, everyone feels right when you—the good guy—win. It teaches an important lesson about how words can hurt. They'll be better people. You can't pay for that kind of lesson . . . but they will.

If someone tells a Polish joke, you're a Polack. Don't be mean about it, just be assertive. Don't laugh; look them in the eye, deadly serious, and tell them that you know they don't really mean what they said, but you find that kind of talk offensive. Being confronted on something like that makes people embarrassed and that's a good thing. People shouldn't make fun of Polacks, and even a stupid Polack should know that by now.

If the remark is about race, tell them your ex-wife is black (or "African-American" or whatever they want to be called that week). If it's about religion, your family is that religion. If it's about women, tell them your daughter was raped and when you went to the trial, the prosecutor said that the rapist had made the exact same comment your friend just made. Then drop it. Don't keep glaring at the insensitive bastard, just focus on cards. If it gets too serious and stays that way, your friend will get defensive and angry. Once you change the feel of the room, it'll be awkward, and that's when you clean everyone out. People won't notice who's winning (you), because they'll be thinking about how uncomfortable the situation is.

Get the moral high ground and then do your dirty work. The guy who made the comment will feel awful. You'll look hurt but appear to put up a front that everything is okay. Everyone else will think there's a lot of tension and be hesitant to look too much at you or the guy who made the comment. They won't want to be involved, so they'll look away. Make the most of it. Use that time.

If this ploy works for you, if you get good at it, stick to men-only games. You can't use this with women at the table. Men act differently around women. They won't make off-color jokes in the first place when females are in the room.

Pick your audiences. If you're in Wisconsin and everyone's making fun of blacks, don't be the one to get upset. If you're in Toronto and they're making fun of people from Quebec, don't bother. If there isn't any high ground, don't try to grab it. Be sensitive, but not prissy. You're standing up for someone's rights, but it has to be someone the others pretend to care something about.

I do this a lot with religion. The only time I've ever been in a church was to play cards in the basement. There's a lot of cash to be made in religion, but I haven't figured out how being religious will make me more money in cards, so I don't follow it. That's also why I don't follow baseball or the stock market.

The followers of Jesus use a fish as their symbol. God's trying to tell you they're fish. Who are you to disobey god?

Getting upset when someone blasphemes can help now and again. There's something about a man with a strong religious conviction (even a bogus one) that commands respect. It's not surprising how many times people scream "Jesus!" or "Christ!" during a game. I always say, "Jesus wouldn't be happy with that." And sometimes I throw in, "He died for our sins." Once I've said that, I make sure there are plenty of sins for him to have died for. I add a few more sins right there at the table while everyone is looking down in quiet reflection. Why should the poor fucker have died in vain?

I went hiking once (I had a good lead on a game). I "bumped into" four accountants (with money) in the lodge. All four were Jewish, of course. Like me, they had gotten tired of walking around in the bugs after the first half day and the old lodge where we were staying didn't have much in the way of entertainment. I led one of them to suggest a poker game by the lantern light and I got it up to a $500 buy-in.

One of the accountants said, "Jesus fucking Christ!" when, through what must have been sheer luck, I beat his nut flush with a full house on the river. I said, "Jesus wouldn't be happy with that kind of talk." The accountant froze like a deer in the headlights and stammered an apology. I nodded and gave him a forced small smile and looked down. I didn't immediately pull in the pot I'd just won. It was all hanging out there. He could see he hurt me.

"I'm sorry, I'm too sensitive at times; it's just that blasphemy really offends me," I said. "I'm sure you didn't mean anything by that."

By saying that, I took away the chance for *him* to say that he didn't mean anything; once I've said it for him, everyone thinks that I think he *did* mean something by it. It was beautiful.

I got lucky the next hand when one of the other accountants said, "Thank god," after someone handed him a beer. I looked at him, perfectly still, then slowly shook my head a bit. I excused myself for about three minutes and let them work each other up. I sat down and took all their money in the next fifteen hands. It was okay for them to lose money to me, because they felt guilty.

Yup, I won money by making Jews feel guilty. I told you this shit was easy.

I knew I'd never play with those guys again, and I got as much out of them as anyone could. None of them were planning to lose $500, yet all four did. That's two grand for me during a shitty vacation in the woods. Not bad. We were never going to be in that stinking lodge together again, and they'd never play with me again, anyway. Not because I cheated (they never knew about that), but because I was too sensitive, and it made them uncomfortable. For that one night, they respected my deep religious beliefs, and they felt wrong for insulting me. All things being equal, it's better to leave behind a bunch of players that don't want to play with you because they think you're too easily offended, instead of a bunch of angry Jews that you bilked out of the money they stole from their clients.

Don't ever try this offended bullshit on me.

Chapter 18

TIPS AND TRICKS

Lawn herbicides took monthly applications to get rid of the weeds, but we still had to deal with the boll weevils," I said. Hamhock glared at me for not playing fast enough, and Twatsie was only half-listening as she stared at her hole cards. Blocky and Gomer were listening to me, but only politely. Any time I talk about my (fake) job as a horticulturist, I can put the room to sleep. No one knows what a horticulturist is, and they wouldn't ask about the work because they wouldn't want anyone else to know that they didn't know.

I took a look at my cards: fishhooks. I could read the nail marks from across the table, but people would have noticed if I didn't at least peek at the faces.

"There's the Carolina boll weevil and the Georgia boll weevil. They're both tough little buggers to deal with and they eat up the crops. Oh, is it my turn to act? Who's dealing?" I asked, looking around the table. I knew exactly who was dealing; I was in the cutoff seat because I dealt the last hand. That was one of the reasons I was sitting with five-sixths of the chips at the table.

"Shut the fuck up and bet!" yelled Hamhock, mostly kidding, but a little bit pissed off.

"Jesus wouldn't be happy to hear that kind of language. Is that really necessary?" I said, mostly kidding, but with some disapproval. He rolled his eyes and fiddled with his chips, but he was down to nubbins.

"So anyway," I said, "one of my guys asks me which of those pests is the harder one to deal with and I say that all boll weevils are tough to control, but I'd rather take on the Carolina variety any day, because . . . it's definitely the lesser of two weevils."

I gave a big smile, and my stupid fucking joke hit Gomer like a sledgehammer in the face. His scotch (from the bottle I brought for him to share with the others) dribbled out of his mouth and he almost convulsed with laughter. Blocky and Twatsie started to laugh hard, too, but mostly at Gomer. Hamhock just snorted and rolled his eyes, but he was distracted by the spewed spit that Gomer got on his shirt.

I laughed, too. I grabbed the king, ace, jack, and queen that I'd been holding out on my lap for the last hour, palmed them, and dropped them on top of the deck as I leaned over and gave Gomer a buddy-slap on his arm. No one saw the move. No one ever sees the move.

I'd already checked the marks on the other players' cards. Ace-nothing for Gomer. He'd play any two, so he might have cum in his pants with an ace in his hand. Twatsie had a 7–8 suited and she'd probably fold. She folded to any bet anyway, and she'd lost most of her stack to the blinds. Blocky had a 3–7 but he was wide open after I busted his straight with a flush in the last hand. That left Hamhock, who was getting tired and hadn't had a winning hand in hours. He had German virgins, 9-9.

Gomer burned a card and showed the flop; what do you know, it was ace-jack-queen. I could see the other aces sitting in the deck, so they couldn't hurt me. I had three jacks. There was no flush draw for Twatsie, so I knew she was probably out. I guessed Blocky would play the hand thanks to tilt, and Gomer was definitely in with a pair of bullets.

"Hey, look at the time. I really should have been home to the wife a few hours ago. This is my last hand for the night," I said. It was 4:30 A.M. and I wanted to wash this game clean in the next five minutes. Blocky was already in the hole for $400 he borrowed from Twatsie. There were three large on the table that weren't part of my stack, and I wanted it all. I hoped that saying it was the last hand would keep Gomer from betting too big on the flop and scaring Twatsie out of the pot too soon. It worked. Small bets, and everyone called.

I saw the next card on top of the deck was a nine. That would have given Hamhock a set, too; it was too bad that card would get burned before the turn. I didn't want to try to pad the stub a second time in one hand, but I couldn't resist and it was the only gamble I took all night. Besides, the dealer was wasted on the cheap scotch I brought him. I asked Hamhock to pass me some snacks, and under the cover of my arm as I reached across the table, I made a sloppy stab at the deck and kicked out the bottom card, which I got on top of the nine before anyone looked at me. I almost flipped the fucker over. That would've looked bad; Gomer goes to deal and there's a card faceup on the deck that was facedown a second before. What the hell, it was worth the risk. I could've told the table I bumped it accidentally if I got caught, but everyone was in their own world right then, and I could've gotten away with anything. A lot of tables won't let you be that bold, but I could have dealt seconds with my cock in this game and no one would've batted an eyelash.

I grabbed a handful of food and moved away from the deck. Gomer burned the new top card and flipped the nine. Now Twatsie had a straight draw. There was another round of low betting; Hamhock decided to try to slow play his set. Good. I bumped up the bet enough to put Twatsie and Gomer all-in. Gomer called—he'd kick his grandmother in the cunt for two aces, so he wouldn't be going anywhere. Hamhock called, even though he had some money left and he should've pushed me all-in. Twatsie folded her straight draw; I figured she might. Blocky pushed all-in with absolutely nothing. He wanted to go out on a win, and he was reading my body language and thought he saw that I was bluffing. I was leaning forward in my seat, and I slammed my chips down when I bet. That must have meant I was bluffing. He had read his poker books. Too bad he hadn't read this one, but I'm sure the others were almost as useful to him.

I looked at Blocky for a long time. I looked at Hamhock. He was the only one left who wasn't down to the felt. I moved all-in; that's more money than anyone had, and I was hoping he would have seen that as a bluff raise. Hamhock called me and pushed his chips to the center. He threw down his nines and I turned over my jacks. The next two cards didn't matter, but I was the only one who knew that fact. I won. I cleaned out three of the four players completely and got Twatsie down to her last dollar. Blocky lost an extra four hundred that he'll have to pay back to another player (for all I cared).

I had known these people for four months, but it was time to go. If this hadn't been my last game with them, I'd have dumped the last hand to Hamhock and made everyone happy. But why lose at all when you'll never see them again? I told everyone I'd see them next week, but I knew I wouldn't. Why would I? They were starting to have money problems—I guess they'd been losing a little more than they could afford to lose over the last few months. What a pity. Tensions were starting to run too high for the game to be profitable, so it was time to leave.

Before I made the Big Mistake, I stayed around some games too long. You've done the work, you know the players, you know how to get to their houses, and you think you can keep sucking that teat until it's dry. No, it's better to leave earlier than later. People are nice when the game is fresh, and I like that. Never outstay your welcome. (See chapter 21, for more on that.)

The little things you do in a game add up. Here's a bunch of them. They'll make cheating a little easier.

Play late at night. The later you play, the better. You'll be a night owl. Not many people play poker at church time on Sunday morning unless they're still playing from Saturday night. It's a nighttime game, and a good game can last for six hours or more. You can sleep in as late as you want—you don't have a job to wake up for. When people get sleepy, they make mistakes; sometimes they'll even try to lose to get a long game to end. They may get edgy, but people are less violent when they're tired and that's the way you want them. They also suffer from eyestrain. They'll misread their own cards, so they'll have no chance of seeing your paperwork. Sleepy players don't protect their cards very well. You'll get more free peeks, and they'll pay attention to other people less so you can work more.

If a game starts before 11 P.M., delay the start as much as you can. Order food, drag your feet. You don't want to play three hundred hands in an evening; you'd rather stall until 1 A.M. and play thirty hands. Fewer hands, bigger pots.

When you play, try to keep the game moving fast. You want to play as many hands in as short a period of time as you can. If you can squeeze in an extra five hands per hour, you'll not only get more pots, but you'll have people making more mistakes. Don't give your friends time to think, but don't nag them to hurry up, either. That will only annoy them. Play fast and make some light jokes about slow players. Lead by example. Fast play also keeps everyone focused on their cards. They won't be thinking about (or watching) you.

Stakes should be pushed up. The bigger the stakes, the more you can take. You should be able to bump the stakes tenfold or more. It's easier to "make things more interesting" when players are tired. It's also easier when the other players are on either winning or losing streaks, or when they're drinking. Winners want to up the stakes because they're doing well; losers want to up the stakes to reclaim their losses.

If you run into tightwads who don't want to bump the stakes, you can propose a *meedle game,* where the stakes are raised only when the players who want to raise them are left in a hand. This keeps one cheapskate from ruining your payday.

Don't be afraid to flash your cards to get extra action. You can flash a red face card to someone sitting next to you, and then swap it out for a black face card. When you turn over your cards to show a club flush, they will think they misread your black card as a red card. Paint cards are hard to tell apart in a quick flash.

There are two types of games you'll play in: long runs and one-shots. In a one-shot game, you'll quickly maximize your take. You'll get in and get out. Maybe there's not much money to be made, or maybe you're just passing through on your way to a regular game. I've traveled all over the country to get into good games, and I never stop looking for action on layovers. You could pick up a whore for the night to kill time, or you could find yourself a one-shot. Which is worth more to you? You're in a town you'll never see again, so there won't be anyone looking for you. It's a great chance to get to know the people of our great country and stick them for all they're worth. One-shot games are good for sharpening your skills—you can push hard and you don't have to be any more friendly and charming than you were to get into the game in the first place. No time is wasted coddling the losers because you'll be gone before they've finished crying.

You can cheat anyone, but younger players and women (if they have the money) are a little safer, and they're less likely to bust you. They haven't been around. Anyone wearing a hat or sunglasses or—god help them—both, has watched a lot of those showboater poker players on TV. They'll think they know the game, and maybe they do. But remember, they don't know your kind of game. Players wearing religious symbols or good-luck charms are my favorites. They've got a "higher power" to blame when things go wrong. They'd be better off handing over their cash and saving you the trouble.

As a matter of fact, they all would.

Chapter 19

CHIPS AHOY!

You're not going to get rich if you only focus on getting the best cards. The object of poker is money, and chips are money. Win the chips or steal the chips, who cares?

You need to handle the cards and the chips the right way. The first baby step of cheating with chips is to put less into the pot than you're supposed to. It's your turn to bet. The bet is $400. You throw $300 into the pot. You splash the pot so no one can see exactly how much you bet.

Use your head. Don't shortchange the pot when you're going to win the hand. There is one person in the world that you don't cheat, and that's you. Don't go light on pots you're going to win. You only go light when you're dumping hands to another player. Minimize the amount you're kicking in for their win.

Let's say you've got six players who each have a $1,000 bankroll. If you plan on coming back to that game on another day, you will rarely want to walk away with all $6,000. Your earnings should be $4,000 to $4,500 on a game like that. You want a couple of the guys to come close to breaking even, a couple of guys to be completely broke, and one other guy (besides you) to be slightly ahead, maybe $1,300. The other winner should win his biggest pot on one of the last hands of the night. Everyone should see his big victory, and they'll remember it.

So the other winner will take in a nice pot, maybe $600. Do you want to give him $600 of your money? Hell no. If you cop one $25 chip out of every hand you dump to another player, that amounts to about $500 by the end of the night. That's good because that's $500 less that you have to be seen winning.

Cop as many chips as you can, but not all from the same pot. You don't want to take a black chip out before the flop, after the flop, after the turn, and again after the river. Someone will notice a pot that's light by $400. But less than $100? Usually not. Especially if the pots are messy. You'll make sure that any neat stacks are accidentally knocked over.

Stay away from *check cop*—that's where you put sticky shit on your hand, like sap or duct tape residue. You put your hand in the pot to drop off some chips and on the way out you stick a chip or two to the bottom of your palm. It's amateurish. It's also an easy way to get caught. I've seen guys do this wrong so chips stick out past the palm. It's hard not to notice when that happens. Learn to palm a chip. It takes practice. Read a coin magic book by a guy named Bobo* to get all the work. Remember to keep your thumb from sticking out. But people aren't looking out for chip coppers, so don't spend too much time worrying about it.

Another good practice is to mix up your chip stacks. Keep low-value chips on top of high-value stacks. Put low-value stacks in front of your big-value stacks. You always want people to think you have less than you have. Make change for bigger chips whenever you can.

* * *

Modern Coin Magic by J.B. Bobo.

In fact, you can make a lot of money by making change out of the pot. When you make a bet for five dollars and you've only got $25 chips, tell the table that you're going to bet five dollars, then put in your $25 chip and take out twenty-five dollars in $5 chips. You've saved yourself the bet. Personally, I like to take out thirty or thirty-five dollars. Again, these are only in pots you're going to lose, otherwise you're increasing the chances of getting caught in order to take money from yourself. Another thing: Don't go making change if you've got the change in your stack.

It's rare that you'll do a chip race in a home game, but if you're playing a freeze-out, sometimes the host will want to do that to keep things tidy. Usually, all the players will get up and stretch their legs while the host or dealer is chipping up. That's a good time to pull part of someone else's stack into your own. Don't grab much unless that guy has just won a big hand and hasn't counted his winnings yet. You should always be watching to see who knows how much they have and who doesn't. Most players have a ballpark idea of how much money is on the felt in front of them, but few players keep an accurate running count.

In general, you don't want to get into any kind of work that takes too much effort. Grabbing chips out of the pot or throwing in fewer than you're supposed to isn't much work. But once in a while, some extra effort can really pay off. Here's a story, and it's even loaded with insider lingo, in case you need something to jerk off to:

I played in a high stakes Limit Hold 'Em game with a bunch of guys near D.C. The host was a guy I'll call Four-Eyes. He was an IRS agent and squarer than a G.I.'s breakfast. He never got tired of making jokes about auditing the other players whenever he beat them in a hand.

Because it was limit poker, we had a lot of raising back and forth. I was playing aggressively and Four-Eyes would never back down. He'd play anything. I was *behind the log* for the first few hours, and I was moving my chips a lot. I *scooted* back and forth with one player who was light. I went cow with another guy. I played banker and sold some of my chips to a couple of latecomers so Four-Eyes wouldn't have to get off his fat ass and give them change. I was digging for more cash after I cashed out early, then I decided to come back in the game and play a few more hands. The whole night was a tidal wave of chips and cash moving through me.

My "lucky streak" ended when my *Little Minnie* got beat by a 7-high straight on the river. I didn't lose that hand graciously, and then I tried to goad Four-Eyes into bumping the limits for a hand. He didn't go for it. I bought some more chips and decided to bring in the next hand for a bet, even though I was sitting on a *gay waiter* (a queen with a trey). A second *mop squeezer* showed up on the flop and I raised the tax man's minimum bet. A king was also on the board. Another king came on the turn and I knew Four-Eyes had *Alabama night riders.* My *four tits* were worthless and I was sitting on a *wooden hand.*

Four-Eyes showed his set of kings and I *duked* my worthless bitches. I threw a little hissy fit and decided I'd cash out. Four-Eyes didn't want me to leave, but I told him I had to get up early to fly to Miami the next morning, so he cashed me out and I left everyone to their game.

I came out ahead by nearly three large in that game. I didn't even bother giving myself good hands. How did I come out ahead? I had played with Four-Eyes one time before; I salted away one of his $100 chips. It was professional quality, 11.5 grams, custom stamped with "Uncle Sam's Casino." How cute. I had a chip manu-facturer print up a stack of 300—they don't ask questions as long as you're not trying to duplicate casino chips. All my work that night was in moving my chips around and going from chips, to cash, to chips again. I snuck in about thirty-five of my counterfeit chips, and no one noticed. When people showed up and wanted to buy into the game, I'd be nice and sell them some of my chips and keep the cash. I'd reach into my pant leg, cop another handful of my replacements, and add them to my stack.

I'm sure the tax man noticed when everyone else tried to cash out hours later. I like to think that the guys who got shorted would accuse Four-Eyes since I never went anywhere *near* his cash box. The tax man couldn't handle basic accounting. What a pity. Fucking a tax man? There are nights when I'm more hero than scumbag. I've never paid taxes in my life and it still felt good.

I spent about $200 to make three grand. I never went to accountant school, but that seems to me like a good return on my investment. I had to buy more counterfeits than I'd ever need, but who cares? Four-Eyes probably figured out what happened, but by that time I was long gone. (And guess what? I wasn't in Miami.)

If you're playing in an Italian game (only red, white, and green chips on the felt), you shouldn't even bother trying to work up an edge on chips. (I don't care about civil rights, but I'm always happy to have blacks at my table.) Copping one extra black chip each half hour will net you an extra unit each night. That's worthwhile. And when mild larceny doesn't work, you've got other skills you can fall back on.

Chip play has been tougher in the last few years, now that a bigger number of bookworms have taken up the game (thanks to television poker and the computer poker games). University boys (especially Orientals) know the math and they think poker is sexy. It never gets their pricks wet, but it's more exciting than algebra. This kind of player takes notes and pays attention, and sometimes they use little calculators to keep track of exactly how much they're up or down. They're also tight-assed, and they might not blow the dust off of their chips for an hour or more before they get a hand they'll play. They might write down each hand and who won it, and they're going to trust their arithmetic more than they're going to trust you (good thinking).

You can still cop chips from these guys. They might be brainy, but they're always pussies. If one notices that you got impossibly lucky or that the pot he won was a few chips light, what's he going to do? E-mail you a virus?

Chapter 20

AVOIDING PROBLEMS

was sitting at a table in Kansas City with four players in a Hi-Lo Seven Stud game. Three of the four players were minnows—Jellyroll, Shithead, and Skippy—and they were in way over their heads. The fourth, Chins, was a sharper who was pulling in almost as much as me and doing it fair and square, the hard-working fool. Chins was The Guy in this part of town. Everyone loved him, and everyone wanted to take him down at the table. When you're the best gunslinger in town, every asshole with a pistol wants to draw on you to make a name for himself. I'm the guy who sneaks into Doc Holliday's hotel room and puts two in his forehead while he sleeps. That's the way to win.

I knew Chins's reputation would wind up fucking me. If I beat him, I'd be seen as a mover. I had to be careful. Every person that played him wanted to beat him, but it happened very rarely. My handing him his ass on a plate would make people suspicious. A stranger rolls in from out of town to clean out the local legend—it could be time for a lynching. Me, I don't even like tight turtlenecks.

Hi-Lo is a good game for winning without being noticed. Take some high pots, some low, and you can do okay without being labeled as the winner. Once in a while you can take both the high and low pots in the same hand, but not too often. I set Chins up to win the other half of every Hi-Lo we played. Even when I wasn't working he was cleaning up, so it wasn't too hard.

I don't begrudge a man his winnings, and more power to him for finding a group of chumps that he could clean out each week. I just hate seeing that much money on the table without getting most of it. The challenge was to get it away from him while keeping him the winner. Jellyroll, Shithead, and Skippy were all-in awe of Chins. They asked his advice on how to play their cards almost every hand. Shit, Jellyroll even showed his cards to Chins in the middle of a play!

I won a couple of big pots off of him—it looked like nothing but an unlucky loss for him, and it confirmed that Chins was as good as everyone thought. I gave him some good cards on my next deal to let him recover some of his losses from the other players. He looked good in front of his groupies, and I stayed under his nose in a close (but unnoticed) second place to pull down a few extra centuries. I made money, but Chins made more.

I could've cleaned him out right then and there (I have my professional pride), but I didn't want a posse coming after me. I had a couple other games a few towns over and I was set to burn those and move on. But I didn't want to leave the area without Chins's money, too.

Skippy gave me the opportunity to come back to that game again and make my move. He'd bullshitted me up at the local pool hall, saying my game was *almost* as good as Chins's. Chins was about to take a trip to Atlantic City to play in a big-money tournament, and this was going to be his last warm-up game. A bunch of people showed up to watch the local hero take me out in a showdown at high noon. We had more than two dozen railbirds for that game. They were making side bets. I was the big underdog.

Chins was getting a *cockle* over me, and all the *chalk eaters* were in on the action. All of these guys played poker, but they wouldn't grow a pecker and sit at the table to play with Chins. They'd just be happy to make side bets that Chins would stick me and the other guys for our buy-ins.

Jellyroll and Shithead weren't happy when Chins wanted to raise the limits, and I fought him a bit, too (just like I'd fight off a stacked 23-year-old blonde waitress who was trying to rape me). Jellyroll was an old buzzard playing with family money, and he didn't even seem to notice the big crowd. He was there to lose and nothing was going to stop him.

It got down to heads-up with me and Chins. I let him do most of the work eliminating the other players, and then I set Chins up to fall hard on one really big hand. He had every reason in the world to believe that his aces and eights would win . . . they didn't. I took all his chips, game over, and I got ready to leave. It was a big win and a big deal. People started to notice how lucky I was and the muttering got louder. Here's the genius: As I cashed out, I gave a C-note to the bookie taking the side bets. I'd put a hundred on Chins winning it all. I congratulated him on his great play, and the ungracious loser said he outplayed me and I just got lucky. Yup, that's me, Lucky Dick.

As my hundred got spread around to the pikers, the grumbling changed. Everyone felt fine with the fairness of my win. What kind of cheating asshole would bet against himself? A cheating asshole who wanted all the money on the table without getting lynched, that's what kind.

I only had the side bet situation come up once in my life, but it shows you where your head needs to be. Always think about where the trouble will come from, and avoid it. It's too costly to get yourself out of trouble once you're neck-deep in it. If you feel like someone is going to ride you hard, don't push him. There's money other places; leave him a few bucks. You don't have to get every red cent from every person at the table every time you play. If you get a really bad loser at your table, let the baby have his bottle. Wipe out only the really good losers. You're looking at the long run. The amount of money and frustration and pain it causes you to get out of trouble is never worth it. You can take risks, and you'll be taking risks every time you make a move, but you want to keep your risks under control.

If you get the choice (and you will), always sit with your eyes on the exit. You want to have a clear idea of the fastest way out of every joint. Usually, you'll draw for seats, and it's easy to track the cards to get the seat you want. You need to know how to get out quick, and you also want to see who might be coming in.

You don't want a latecomer to walk up behind you, slap you on the back, and startle you during a move. You jump, your hold-outs fly up on the table, and you've got a lot of explaining to do. Maybe law enforcement professionals show up. You want to see them coming so you can decide whether to run or use the few extra seconds to put together a good story.

One time, in Arkansas, I was in a roughneck game where three guys with sawed-off shotguns and ski masks crashed the party to hold us up (there were *hundreds* of dollars on the table, high stakes for inbreds). This was a cash-on-the-table game, and when the first gun came through the door, I grabbed as much money as I could and ran out the back before the hicks knew what was happening. I didn't make more than I was going to make by cheating, but I made it faster. I didn't get my brains blown out, I kept all my money and jewelry, and I got my night's pay. I was probably in bed before the robbery was over. I never went back to that game—fuck that. I could've explained my stealing by saying I was saving their money, but then they'd want some of it back. The crooks knew where our game was, the police might have gotten involved, and there wasn't any real money left there. It's also possible that the robbers blew everyone's heads off when they found out there was no money in the game. For all I knew, one of my friends had tipped off the robbers for a piece of their take. Fuck them.

Don't win too much at a game. It's a temptation, but don't be putting on the sizz all the time. Winning every time will make your job harder. You need to have believable luck. You balance your good luck by giving yourself some really bad beats that fuck you hard. One of my personal favorites is to have the board beat all hands, so the pot gets chopped. Your couple pair goes down to a board that's aces full of kings. You don't lose a dime, but everyone remembers that you got fucked out of a big hand. That's bad-beat equity that doesn't cost shit to you. You have to remember that to make your money, you need your beats. Tell a fucking story. Plan it and tell it. Make it good, but make it real. You don't have to be Shakespeare, but make it interesting.

You might get *singed* once in a while—maybe someone will notice a hanger while you're bottom dealing, but only with their peripheral vision. They'll sense something isn't right, but they won't know what. You want to lay low after that. You'll know when this happens because people won't be burning you—they'll look confused instead of angry. They might ask questions to find out whether they saw what they thought they saw. When you get singed, lay off the tricky moves for a while. Use other techniques. Mix it up.

Always keep talking. You're everyone's best friend, and everyone will give you the benefit of the doubt if you play it right. Don't give anyone the upper hand if a situation develops. Take control. If someone calls you out for using a shiner, settle him down. Ask him to be calm and to clearly explain what he's talking about. Take what he says very seriously. You're going to help him figure out what happened. Ask him questions, involve other players, be the solution to the problem. You created it; you can help solve it. When you take control, you take control away from him.

Have some stories ready to go. There shouldn't be apologies or excuses, there should just be stories that will get people thinking about you and feeling sorry for you. You never admit guilt; you want them thinking about something other than the possibility that someone could have been cheating. You want sympathy. Cancer is good. Kids are good. Get that bullshit out there. Maybe you have a hard luck story about how you're down to the tough money and you shouldn't even be gambling, and how your wife is going to leave you. Give them a better story to think about than a cheat ripping off people at a card game (without ever admitting you did that). A young son dying of cancer, a librarian wife brutally raped by a motorcycle gang . . . Put life in perspective for these assholes. There are more important things in life than money and cards.

Any distraction can get you out of a tight spot. I carry animal laxatives to spike a few drinks if I smell trouble coming. It's easy to score, it's not illegal to have on you, and a little bit in their beer will give them something else to think about. But you have to know trouble is coming ten minutes in advance, and if you know that, there should be other ways out. Still, it's easy to carry and it can be a funny way out. You can always call 911 to bust up the games and give the players a tougher situation to worry about. Or fake a seizure. Piss, shit, and vomit will get people to forget about cards and they won't want to touch you. Do anything to stop the word "cheating" from being mentioned and, if it is, don't let it be repeated.

Avoid confrontation. You don't want a gun or a knife fight. Stop trouble before it starts. Turning and walking away works most of the time, but not always. You could get shot in the back. Always know what everyone is thinking, and if they're thinking of fucking you up, get out fast. Just make sure you grab the money on your way.

Chapter 21

BURNING

Y ou'll know when the party's over and it's time to go. You'll know it before you get *rumbled*; if you get rumbled, that's the final hint for the stupid. You'll learn. When someone starts watching you too hard, it's a good time to split. When most of the money has gone from the game into your pocket and people are digging less to keep playing, that's the time to leave. No game lasts forever. The key to being successful in this business (besides cheating) is to know when to get out.

Card games get burned all the time. There's no way to avoid it. I've had games that I've played for years, but they're the exceptions. You can't cheat for cigarette money alone. Cheating is dangerous; you deserve to get paid well for it. You have to make more at cheating than you would by simply being a good player. Your job is much harder than being a good poker player, and it's worth more. Maximize the return on your time.

As you're getting your pecker wet, most of your games will be one-shot hit and runs. Get away from any town you've spent time in. Get to the other side of the country. Get a new name and new clothes. Meet people, be friendly, get in a few games, stuff your pockets as fast as you can, then leave and never look back. It's the best way. Every time you walk back into a room, there's a chance you're walking into a guy with a baseball bat and a good memory. You play, you win, you thank everyone, you make plans to see everyone next week, and you mysteriously disappear. They'll forget about you, and the money doesn't know where it comes from, so it won't remind you.

There's no shame in leaving a game. There's no shame in leaving a little money on the table. Don't expect to get every dime out of every rube you play with; you're not going to get the fillings out of their teeth. You'll get as much as you can get away with. The amount you can get away with goes up the more games you cheat. I can get away with taking everyone for every cent they have on them, but it's hard work. Leave a couple hundred behind and walk out instead of having to run out. It doesn't cost much to be "nice" and you get to keep your face intact. I always lose the last hand of an evening. I'm greedy, but I think of that last hundred bucks as a tip. The guy that wins the last hand thinks his luck is changing and he'll want to come back, and people remember the last hand played. I've said this before and I'll say it again. It's good advice. It seems wrong to let the other players win at all, but it's worth your while.

Knowing when it's time to leave doesn't just mean knowing what *day* to stop playing with a group, but also at what *time* to stop. If you take a monster pot early in the night and people are looking around at each other, you might want to get out of a game sooner than you usually would. Dump a hand to them, tell them you've got to be up bright and early the next day, and get the fuck out of Dodge. They can't beat you up if they can't find you.

If you wait too long, it's much harder to get out. Once people accuse you of cheating, you're in a world of shit. You have to think fast and work hard. It's not worth the energy. Once you've got a sign on your back, you have a lot to worry about, and none of that extra work or anxiety is going to bring you another dime. You don't want to increase your work without increasing your money.

Be ready to go at all times. Home is wherever you are. Home is in your pockets. Home is your money. When you go to a city, never unpack your bags. You can stay at a hotel, but don't leave anything there that you need or want. That's better left in your car. Your car can move with you. I keep some personal items in my hotel room. If people find out where you live (if they do, you fucked up), and if they come looking for you (if they do, you really fucked up), you want them to figure that you're still in town when you're not. Maybe it's your friends looking for you, or maybe it's the law. If they see stuff still in your room, they figure you're coming back. I keep a box full of shaving kits, undershirts, and sets of keys in my trunk. The keys sell it. You can go to a locksmith and buy a box of keys—car, home, whatever. Put them on a ring with a little keychain and have several sets. Keep a bogus set with you and a bogus set in your room. Keep your real car key off the chain and in a different pocket. That's the only key you'll need.

I sometimes get up and stretch my legs when things look like they could get unpleasant. I leave my set of keys right on the table where everyone can see them. It'll take the smart ones half an hour to figure out those keys are fakes, and you won't meet many smart ones. That's forty miles in a direction they can't guess, and you won't waste time going back to your hotel.

Watches, cigarette cases, small suitcases, and cell phones are great personal items to leave in a place when you want people to think you'll be coming back. They cost you next to nothing to buy, and they can buy you valuable time to bug out. You can steal some of this stuff, but it's hardly worth it—a pawn shop is cheap and easy. They should look used, anyway. A brand new set of keys will look like a brand new set of keys. Leave them out, get them dirty.

These items should look like they're important to you. Put a fucking rabbit's foot on it. Leave a wallet with photographs and fake credit cards in it.

If you're in the middle of a game and things look sour, a great out is to get up for a cigarette. You can leave your keys, your jacket, even your shoes. You step out on the porch for a smoke, and hit the trail. If you have a bad feeling, act on it. You can always use a smoke—and what better place to smoke than in your car on the open highway, heading toward the next game of your life?

Always keep your car gassed up and know the quickest way out of town. You might have to leave in a hurry, and you don't want to have to stop at the fucking Mobil station to ask how to get to the highway. Know your way around, and know one back-up route, too.

In a small town, you'll want to have maps, food, and probably an extra can of gas in your trunk. It's not likely that law enforcement professionals will set up a ten-mile dragnet for a suspected poker cheat, but sometimes they have nothing better to do. You shouldn't be as worried about the law as you should be about pissed-off friends.

Don't get attached to the idea of big wins. If you're in a game for several weeks and you're planning to take it down in one fell swoop, you always have to be ready to ditch it. Staying around for an extra week or two when there's too much heat will get you hurt. One way you avoid that is by taking five hundred a week from a game until you're ready for the Main Event, when you'll take them for ten large. If you have to leave town early, you at least made beer money.

When it's time to go, just *go*. Six weeks in a town will give you enough time to find the games, build them, and burn them; but you might have to leave earlier. Don't question it. You might get a hard-working asshole job to get closer to a big-money game, and you might have a hard time leaving before getting your pay. You might be getting some tail from a local waitress and not want to leave her behind. You have to be ready to disappear in the middle of the night and never contact anyone in that town again. Always be ready to go.

You can have a phone or a beeper or a mobile phone. When you leave, those get left behind, too. Did you leave clothes at the dry cleaner? Forget them; you'll make enough money to buy more. Are you supposed to play golf the next day? Too bad. Nothing keeps you in town. "Good-byes" will get your ass kicked for you.

Even if you burn a game and it seemed like smooth sailing, don't spend the night in town. Drive as far as you can that night and rent a motel room. Do you want one of your fish spending twelve hours thinking about how they lost their money? Do you want to bump into him the next day as you're loading up your car to leave? Why risk it? Once you've made up your mind that it's time to go, don't dawdle. Get the fuck out.

If you finish a game after winning a freeze-out, make sure that you've talked about upcoming events. Plan dinner with all the wives. Set up a time to go bowling. Start a fucking business with someone. You want everyone thinking about the next time they'll see you, and then they can fantasize about winning their money back (and then some). Don't make up any bullshit excuses for why you won't be around. As far as they know, they will be seeing you again soon. Don't tell them you won't be around because you're going on a business trip. You don't have to explain why you won't be around, because you're never coming back to explain. They won't get to ask you. I'd bet that most games I burn keep a seat open for me the next week (after I'm long gone), figuring I'm just running late.

Sometimes you'll get to liking a couple of people, and you might have the crazy idea that you can stay in touch with them. You might think that you can trust them. No. Even if they aren't in your poker group. Even if you never talked poker. No. People talk. Sometimes there are hidden connections. Don't risk it.

I'm sure I've burned a lot of games before I had to. I used to look back and regret it, until that one time when I stayed too long. Now I know it's much better to walk away from a game with money on the table than to stay too long and wind up chewing dirt.

Remember: When you leave, no one knows you're leaving. Don't even think about it. Don't fuck up and give anyone an idea that you're splitting. Don't say, "Good luck with everything" on your way out the door. Say, "See you soon." Say, "See you next week." Let them plan on that. You'll be somewhere else and won't even remember their names. Don't worry about them having good luck—you leaving town is the best luck they're going to hit for a long time.

You're General Sherman, and you leave nothing behind but some car keys and aftershave (did Sherman do that?). No friends, no feelings, no nothing. Just burning cities that you can never go back to. The good news is that there are plenty of places to go. It's a big, beautiful country, and you've got plenty of matches.

Chapter 22

CORING THE APPLE

Most of the games you'll find won't be big ones. Every once in a while, you'll get yourself in a nice game that will bring you five large for a night's work. But if you do your schmoozing job right, you may find yourself invited to an *apple*—a big-money game ripe for picking.

These games will have the same players week in and week out. The players have fancy-ass jobs and much more money than they deserve or need. No one will really care about winning or losing the money (yeah, sure); they'll only care about losing face. A real apple will earn you fifty or a hundred grand in one night. They may only play once every couple of months, or even just once or twice a year.

It's a lot of work to get yourself into a real big-money game. It took me three years to get to the table of a game hosted by a judge in New Hampshire. I'd heard people talking about that game in a home game in North Carolina, so I headed up to sniff around. Poker players talk, and one of the players in the Big Game also played in some local card rooms, bragging about how he won a $30,000 pot. Most people would hear that and think the guy was blowing smoke up their asses, but I know these games exist. I nosed around, found the town where Judge lived, and I stopped by the country club. I wasted a couple months there. I got in a couple of nickel-and-dime games to make my nut, but no one I met talked about the Big Game.

I didn't give up. I went back to New Hampshire whenever I could, even though it's a barren poker wasteland. I kept sniffing. I knew that game would be worth the effort, and I was right. (I often am.)

I found out that one of the players was a big television executive in Houston. I knew I couldn't get close to Judge, so I went after Mr. TeeVee. They were hiring at his station for a high-level job. I took a copy of their ad and reposted it in Austin using a post office box as the return address. That got me a bunch of tapes from people who wanted TV work. I picked the best one, then paid a kid at a community college to edit the creator's name off of the tape. I pumped up one of the resumes, added my name, and I applied for the job in Houston. I bought a pricey suit and a briefcase, and I had a damned interview. I dropped Mr. TeeVee's name and weaseled my way in to meet him.

He was the head honcho, so using his name won me some points. I didn't care. I just needed to press palms and get his card. We chatted for a few minutes and I casually mentioned that I'd been wanting to do a big TV project involving poker. His eyes lit up. Hey, guess what? He played all the time! Well, goddamn. We swapped stories and slapped each other on the back a few times. I slipped him a Cuban, and by the end of my time in Houston I had his business card with all his personal numbers written by hand on the back.

The station called me to ask for references and to set up another interview a few days later, but I pulled my application. Fuck them. I could have scammed an "honest" job in television. Give me a break. I am a cheat, but I do have standards.

I called up Mr. TeeVee to personally tell him that my freelance business was going too well to take the job (it sure was), but I'd still love to meet up and talk about poker. I met him in Houston a few times over the next year to play in his home game. That alone would have been a pretty good score, but I didn't take much from it, just enough for expenses. I buddied up real cozy with him; he was my ticket to the Big Game. Patience.

We'd talk politics and sports and we agreed on everything. He could've changed his mind on every topic of conversation and I'd have still agreed with him. We stayed off the subject of television. I didn't like to talk about "work," and I didn't know jack shit about what he thought I did for a living. He was still trying to get me to come work with him in Houston. He kept sweetening the offer. If I weren't morally opposed to fair work, I would have been tempted. All I know about television is that if you show up in a suit with a videotape and a cigar, they'll hire you. On more than one occasion, he'd thank me for advice when I never spoke a word. He didn't deserve the money I was going to take from him.

Mr. TeeVee never mentioned the Big Game. Without being too obvious, I was always trying to get the topic to come up. I played in his games for two more years before he mentioned off the cuff that he was going to New Hampshire in the fall.

Oh, I love it up there. Did he know I had family just one town over from where Judge lived? I had planned to be up there in the fall, too . . . what a strange coincidence! He was thrilled. He didn't want to push me, but might I be interested in a game with bigger stakes? He really didn't want to put me on the spot, but there was a judge up there who had eight regulars twice a year for a "pretty big money game." No shit? He'd mentioned me to Judge a few times, and, as it turned out, one of their regulars was going to be overseas in the fall, so there was a seat open. I told him I'd think about it, but it sounded good. How big was "big money"? Really? Oh, I guess I could handle that—business was good. It was about to get much better.

I was in. I showed up at Judge's house. He did it up right. First-class snacks, a five-thousand-dollar poker table, custom chips, and a professional dealer from one of the Indian casinos. Okay, so I'd have to work for my money, but the stakes were huge. I wasn't going to burn this game; it could be a cash cow for a while. I did a little bit of nail marking and some subtle advantage play, and that alone was enough to net me $60,000 my first night. More important, I made nice with all the players: Judge, Cappy, Mr. TeeVee, Blinky, Stretch, Alkie, and Boomer. Each of them thought I was as charming as Satan. And each of them was worth millions. It got their little peckers hard to lose a few hundred grand and remind themselves they could afford it. Most of them flew in on their private jets just for the game. They all couldn't have been happier losing money to one of their own. Fuck them.

I could've worked that game over hard. If I'd cleaned each of them out for everything on the table, it would have been well over 250K. I could have rung in a cold deck with that dealer, right under his nose, but I wanted to keep this game. No one else could work it. It was mine. They were all mine. I worked that game once or twice a year for six years and took out more than two million bucks. That's all you have to do. That's a fine living.

But you need to be smart. I didn't win every session. I dumped twice, never losing more than a quarter of my smallest win. But when I lost, everyone remembered it. I was never a bad sport, because no one wants to play with a sore loser. I lost on really bad beats, unbelievable streaks of bad luck. The two times I lost were talked about for years. Everyone at the table, including the winners (once Boomer and once Judge—it's always good to give your host some complimentary play), all felt bad for me. I was gracious. I netted more than two million in six years (which makes it a hell of a lot easier to be gracious), but if you asked any of them, they'd only remember my two "big" losses.

When you find the apple, take good care of it. Don't talk about the Big Game at your smaller games. You don't want anyone else sniffing around, trying to get in. The thing to remember in those huge-money games is that they won't let just anyone in. You need to have a connection. They have to really trust you. You may have to work it for a long time. And they'll only want to play with guys that they like to pal around with at the table. The guys in the premium games are hardworking rich scumbags and they all have the same personalities. They're not that different from you; they're professionals, and they don't have real friends, but they want buddies. You've got to be what they want. It's comradarie. You won't talk about work. You'll cheat at poker and everyone will love you for it.

I never got into too many regular games. In general, I like to take as much money as I can, then take off. The trouble with regular games is that the longer you stick around, the better the chances you'll get busted. If you play a regular game, you can't clean everyone out each week or the game will fall apart. But those premium games are worth sucking on for a few years.

I worked my way into another big game in L.A. (Los Angeles, not Louisiana). It was a celebrity's home game. This little fellow (movie stars are short!) has been hosting one of the best-known Hollywood games for almost twenty years. He only invites other Hollywood types. They aren't all actors—there are plenty of producers, accountants, and agents that no one has ever heard of who play—but some fairly big stars come out, too.

Now, I don't care two shits on a Thursday about celebrity. The best thing about famous people is that they have some coin and they want everyone around them to know it. Their losses are easy come, easy go—what's another Hummer?

I got invited to sit in on this celebrity's game after I took a guy (who turned out to be one of his semi-regulars) for $7,500. He thought I was a pro (I am) and he wanted to see me take a few of the stars down a few pegs. He introduced me as a guy "in the biz" and I played in that game seven or eight times. The money was pretty good, but to listen to those fuckers go on and on about themselves, their "art" (fucking jiggle shows), and their "responsibility to society" made it a lot of work just to keep my lunch down. The pots never got as high as I like, but it was a great way into other games in Malibu and Beverly Hills. Once people knew I played with that group of famous people, they wanted to play with me. I guess it made me "hip."

That game was an apple for me because it led me to a lot of other games that were easy pickings. I never burned that game, but I got sick of dealing with the asshole Californians. Jesus Christ (and I took some of that money, too), it's a lot of work. When you find a big game, don't try to squeeze it dry; you can make a lot in the long haul, and sometimes you can make more from the other games it leads to. A lot of losers in a group may play with other losers on other nights. These fish swim in schools.

If you ever do play with famous people, remember that they've got huge fucking egos. No kidding. They don't like to lose and they're always "better than average" in their own minds. They pay people to tell them that, but still, you have to tell them, too. Always dump to them on the last hand so they remember they're winners. They are winners. The world is their oyster. It's the good life. They

134 How to CHEAT Your FRIENDS at POKER

love the attention. For me, all the money I took out just wasn't fucking worth it. You can go in and take those games if you want. Maybe you want to feel like you're in with the in crowd. Personally, the only time I want an autograph from one of those losers is when it's at the bottom of a personal check.

Chapter 23

TAKE THE MONEY AND RUN

Never forget why you're sitting at the table: Money. You want the money any way you can get it. Any loan you won't pay back is fair game. So is a cheating side bet. You shouldn't even be thinking about fair—you're a cheat. Wring the game dry, and then move on to the next one. Wring the town dry, and move on to the next one.

If you've got qualms about getting the money, you're going to have problems with this chapter. And if you have problems with this chapter, it's your fault for buying the book. Black legs get a little dirty sometimes.

You walk into a *Z-game* you've been hanging around for a few weeks. It's penny-ante bullshit. You've been watching the game like a vulture, pushing as hard as you can to get them to play for some real money. No one bites. They all have plenty of money, but they're too fucking cheap to raise the limits. You take home a yard if you're lucky. You stick around because you hope it'll get better and there's no other game in this town.

Then one day you walk in the front door and take off your coat. The guys are in the living room playing their pissant little game, and before you even shout "Hi, boys!" you see the host's wife has left her purse on a small table in the foyer. No one's there, so you take a little peek into her wallet. Six hundred bucks cash. That's more than you'll ever clear out of this game. You grab the whole wallet, stuff it in the front of your pants, grab your coat, and leave. You never talk to any of the players again and you get out of town right away. You don't just take the cash because you want her to wonder whether her pocket was picked. If you know someone who will give you a few bucks for the plastic, you flip it (otherwise just toss it in the trash somewhere). It's six bucks you were never going to see in the game. Seize the day, grab the wad, hit the road.

That's stealing. Absolutely. It's illegal. Guess what? So is cheating at poker. Stealing just doesn't *feel* right to you. Well, cheating at poker won't either, at first. But as you get better at it, you'll get used to the feeling. If you're going to do it, do it all the way. Pinching a wallet, marking a card: they're the same thing. Branch out when it's easy. You're not going to start putting on ski masks and breaking into houses. You're not going to rob. You're not going to hurt or scare anyone. You're never going to hit anybody. But you should take advantage of every opportunity that falls into your lap. It's what you do.

If you saw a C-note lying on the road, would you take it? Would you look around to make sure no one saw you? Would you ask anyone if they dropped it? Or would you just grab it and stuff it in your pocket and walk away? Of course you would. If you see the money, you take the money. Never do extra work. That six hundred out of the purse *lowers* the chances of getting busted or hurt. It's easier and safer for everyone.

The game's bank is also a fair target. I've wasted my time in worthless little games that didn't get above two-dollar maximum bets, but the host kept a grand or two in his little lockbox. When the timing was right, I grabbed the box and went out the back way. I was going to give up anyway, so why not be paid for my time? Get the biggest take as quickly as possible, then move on.

Don't make a money grab if they can figure out right away that it was you. You want a big head start. Don't go to the bathroom, grab the bank, and climb out the window. You'd be gone too long, and that can get the cops called before you're out of town. If no one can be sure it's me, I'll do anything. At the end of the game when everyone is leaving, maybe I grab the box. It'll take a while to figure out who did it. They'll figure it out after a few weeks when I'm the only one who doesn't come back; but I work the friendly and trust-worthy angles, so no one is going to suspect me first. I don't even look like I need the money. I don't need the money. I *want* the money. I take the money.

If you broke into a bank, stole all the money, and then gave it to charity, would you be a bad guy or a good guy? No one with money in the bank is going to go hungry. If they needed the money to eat, they wouldn't have it in the bank because they'd be spending it on food. It's extra money. The bank can afford to lose the money. What if the bank left the money in bags outside? People would take it. If people don't want their cash taken, they should keep it in a place out of easy reach. Anyone who plays poker wants their cash taken, and it doesn't matter how you do it.

Be creative. Have fun with your life. I played in a weekly game with a bunch of thirty- to forty-year-olds who worked at a north-eastern college. One night, three young coeds showed up shitfaced. They'd heard about the game and wanted to play some poker. They weren't beauties, but they were all fuckable. They were welcomed into our game. Somebody suggested, only half-jokingly, that we play strip poker. After a few more drinks the girls agreed, and no one had to convince the fellows.

We played for six hours. I won big. All the girls were completely naked and ready to play for "favors." The guys were down to socks and underwear. I told the table that I was taking my winnings, then scooped up all the clothes and walked out of the room. Everyone had a good laugh. Besides, no one was going to chase me across campus in just their underwear, and with a raging hard-on.

I went out the back door, got into my car, and drove away. I never saw my friends again. They must have thought of it as a joke taken way too far. They were drunk and never thought to stop me; they must have forgotten that I had all of their wallets in their slacks. It was strange happenstance that that particular poker day was payday; they each had a lot of cash ready for poker that night.

Subtract the $300 I'd paid the hookers to pose as coeds, (and subtract the "Rolex" I gave to the one that stayed friendly after the game), and it was still a good business move. Whores can act; they almost had me believing they were shy about taking off their clothes. When I met them to give them back their clothes and the rest of their money, they were still very friendly. I made them all promise not to tell anyone. Shhh.

The guys had the time of their lives. I saved them a trip to Vegas, and the lap dancers there would have charged more money to show tits that wouldn't have been as nice. They (and I) got their money's worth.

Chapter 24

GAMES PEOPLE PLAY

My *Lord went thins* on me during a long trip to work every Elk lodge I could find. It seemed like a good idea: The B.P.O.E. is a "fraternal society" that does charity work, talks about Jesus, and gives some of its members a chance to get shitfaced at their regular meetings. They have thousands of clubs across the country just filled with guys who are hiding out from their dull lives. Their dull lives have no trouble finding them. Rich people don't sign up for this club, but there are plenty of members with enough money to make it worthwhile.

B.P.O.E. is supposed to stand for "Benevolent & Protective Order of Elks" but I think of it as "Biggest Pricks on Earth." Who cares about an old fart with a moose on his shirt? But they're all religious, bonding and drinking, and that's a great environment for poker. They have private clubs with back rooms, and law enforcement professionals leave them alone.

I thought about joining the Elks, but instead I grabbed a membership card off of a friend. We played in a regular game together, and he'd tell stories about his monthly Elk club adventures. He got me thinking on the idea, and since he brought it up, I took his card.

I decided to travel around a few states, drop over to see my "brother" Elks, and offer up the chance to play some cards (if no one was playing already). I'd make every stop a one-shot deal, and I'd hit as many clubs as I could in two months. My name (the name of my friend on the membership card) wouldn't get around that fast, and I figured that Elks probably didn't migrate from lodge to lodge, so I wouldn't get busted.

There were fewer games going on than I expected. What the fuck else do they have to do? Sit around and talk about how swell god is? You have to practice to make meetings this dull. They sit and talk about helping people, they agree with each other, but they don't do anything. That makes them feel good about themselves, I guess, but I had really bad luck trying to start up games. I'd say "poker" and a lot of people would laugh, like it was some kind of exotic fancy-pants game from a far-off land. I figured maybe my personality intimidated the Elks, but that wasn't it; they just weren't eager for a highfalutin game with their "brother" from another lodge.

Gambling was happening at all of these places. It was usually hidden. People would swap a fin back and forth after a ball game, but it was under the table. They'd play cribbage and backgammon for money, but it was hushed up. It was a private club, but they were embarrassed to bet on anything, like they had something else they were supposed to be doing. What is gambling, some fucking sin?

It took a while, but my luck finally changed when I got them playing some other card games. From there, I eased into poker. At that point, I was throwing valuable time after shit money, but I wanted to make something off those old coots. No chips, just playing on the nose. After some Hearts or Oh Hell (I wish to Christ I was kidding), I'd ask around for what other games people knew. Good Americans know a lot fewer games than you'd think. I'd let them keep calling out games until someone mentioned poker.

Most of these useless fucks don't even know how to play real poker. There were usually barely enough of them to get a game going. Everyone knew some stupid bullshit variation of poker, so I spent most of my time not playing any Draw, Stud, or Hold 'Em . . . I was playing all the idiot games that only the worst piker will bring up at a "dealer's choice" home game. I learned a lot, and maybe someday what I learned will pay off—if I want to cheat in the fucking old folk's home.

You may have a devil of a time getting the stakes high in idiot games. If your players aren't serious enough to play a real game, they won't play for real money. The nice thing about poker is that a full house is always a full house, and it's always better than a flush (you might have to explain that to a couple of Elks). All the mechanics are the same, but when you skip from one bullshitty game to another, you spend more time teaching the players which cards are wild than you do taking their bullshit money.

I probably should've given up on the Elks after the first couple of lodges I played in, but I was making gas money and I was learning the Elks. Now that I know them, I can make a bit of money without much work wherever they have a lodge. The nice thing about a group of people is that most members of any given group are the same wherever you go. Learn it once and you don't ever need a refresher course. People who become Elks are religious, boring, boozehounds, and high-and-mighty. Most don't gamble, but enough of them do that I can always find some low-rent game to get me to the next town. You might feel like a fool when you're cheating people at kiddie games, but the money's still green.

No one lost even a hundred bucks. But, each meeting had between seventy-five and a couple hundred members. People would play a game for twenty dollars cash, lose it, not sweat it, and then go drink Manhattans and talk about Flag Day. Instead of taking five people for $400 each, I was taking 100 people for twenty dollars each. It was good exercise. Fucking Elks.

You need to know as many varieties of poker as you can. Any time a loser wants to stop playing stud and try a round of Blind Man's Bluff, take him up on it. People will play one or two hands of that, and you'll be done. The only good thing about these variations is that real poker players won't care about them and they'll gripe and grumble about wasting their time. No one will pay attention to who wins. Since the winner will be you, it's free money. They don't know enough to catch you and they wouldn't know what to do with you if they did.

After a long night, I'd know who the "real" players were. None of them could play, but I'd know who thought they could. I'd set them up for a home game, or play into the wee hours for a few hundred extra.

Learn California, Lamebrain Pete, Utah, Crazy Pineapple, High Chicago, Pig in the Poke, High Mambo, Kansas City Lowball, Kankakee, American Filthy Monk, Spit in the Ocean, Rembrandt, Screwy Louie (or Anaconda, or Pass the Trash), Lazy Pineapple, Seven-Toed Pete, Cincinnati, Wild Annie, Two of Three, Two-Twenty-Two, Tennessee, and No Peeky.

When you learn all those games, you'll find out that a lot of them are the same game with different names. You'll also learn that different people have different ideas about what the rules of the game are. This puts you in a good position, because you'll be the authority once you can tell them the difference between Little Virginia and Razzle Dazzle. You could win all the money just by adjusting the rules to your favor and using their honest readers. Make up rules to get more money on the table. Tell them that a pair of aces means you can double the betting limit the next hand—then give yourself aces.

I hate them, but don't turn your back on the kiddie games. Money on the table is money in your pocket. If you see a game of bridge for $500, take it. Give yourself enough paint and you'll win big. People who like the poker variations only want to play "for fun"—but if that's what they're playing, play it. People play more and lose more when they're having fun. If a guy with a lot of cash wants to play Lazy Pineapple and a tightwad insists on Five-Card Draw, go with the money.

Another thing you're going to run into is freak hands. For whatever reason, when people play with pelters, they often forget (or don't know) what beats what. You can read the charts to see the odds on getting these hands (*see* the appendix on page 243), but when you play enough, you'll just know. Play a million hands of poker and you'll know that two pair is more common than a straight.

The ranking of hands from highest to lowest (without wild cards), including freak hands, is:

1.	royal straight flush	11.	full house
2.	skeet flush	12.	little tiger
3.	straight flush	13.	little dog
4.	four aces	14.	five and dime
5.	blaze full	15.	big cat
6.	big bobtail	16.	big dog
7.	four of a kind	17.	flush
8.	blaze	18.	skeet (aka pelter)
9.	round the corner straight	19.	skip straight (aka Dutch straight or kilter)
10.	little bobtail	20.	straight

21.	four flush with pair	24.	two pair
22.	three of a kind	25.	pair
23.	four flush	26.	no pair

A lot of Elmers out there like to combine freak hands with stupid poker games. When someone wants eights and suicide kings wild in a game of Holy Nun Limit Heartaches with a twist, be ready for them. Usually those players are in the minority, and you won't want to piss off the real players to make one guy happy. But the majority rules. I'll play Go Fish for the right price. I'll win, too.

Most of the time with the Elks and their ilk, you're probably better off just siphoning the gas out of their cars and driving to a real poker game somewhere else.

Chapter 25

TAKING THE HIT

D on't think about cards or people, think about money. That must be your focus. GTM: Get The Money. That's why you're playing cards. That's why you're talking to people. That's your only job. If you enjoy cheating, time will fly by, but always keep in your head why you're playing. Never ease up on someone because you like them. These are not really your friends. They want to lose money on poker and you're just there to help them. Your service doesn't include real friendship; they can't afford that. Does a pro boxer skip around the ring because he likes or—god forbid—respects his opponent? No. Go in for the kill, do your job, get out, move on. In the long run, everyone will be happier.

There's a very close second in your rule book to Get The Money and that's DGFC: Don't Get Fucking Caught! Ever. Getting caught is never a good idea, and no matter what you've heard, it's not a part of the cheater's life. Boxers avoid getting knocked out at all costs. Don't take getting caught lightly. It's not something you shrug off because "it happens." It shouldn't happen. If you're getting busted, you're doing something wrong. Boxing isn't the best example to compare to cheating, but if you think that getting caught could be a part of your everyday cheating life, you'll be kissing the canvas . . . literally.

Airplanes crash once in a while, but you don't learn to fly a plane by trial and error. Think of cheating at home games the same way. Think about what you've read in this book and decide that you're going to do it. Do all the work, learn the lessons, and don't just practice the moves—make them a part of you. Then start slow. Feel your hands tremble, taste the sick coming up the back of your throat, and feel the sweat soaking your armpits (your first time out, wear a suit coat). It gets easier, but don't let it get too easy. The trembling, the vomit, and the sweating will go away, but don't kick back and think you can't be caught. If you're busted, the shaking, vomiting, and sweating will all be back. Getting caught feels like skydiving, but you don't want to get off on it. Don't get cocky and think you can handle it.

I met a guy, Rocky, who used to be a heavyweight boxer in Chicago. He was big, bald, ugly, and mean, and he liked playing cards. Rocky told me why he quit boxing. He realized he wasn't getting into the ring to win. He didn't even care about hitting other guys. He was going into the fight to be punished. Rocky kept fighting because he liked getting hit. When he realized that, he quit.

I used to feel the same way once in a while. Looking back on it, every time I've gotten busted, some part of me wanted it to happen. I'd get horny for a beating. My life got too square sometimes, and I wouldn't want to forget that I'm an outlaw. I needed to remember that I wasn't one of the hardworking assholes I rip off. I wanted to feel my heart pounding and maybe spit some blood, then crawl off and lick my wounds. It worked better than smelling salts.

I'm writing this so you learn. You don't want to get caught. Don't let that sickness grow in you. If you want to feel like a bad boy, go give head to a sailor in a bus station. It's a better way to feel dirty than getting your hands broken. You don't have to get kicked in the balls to prove you have them.

The only reason to risk getting caught is money. If the payout is high enough, you can go out on a limb. But you have to be honest with yourself (never with anyone else; always with yourself). If you're not cheating for the money and *only* for the money, take a few days off. Get laid. Read a book. Get drunk. Get it together before someone gives you what you're begging for.

Never get caught in a low-stakes or a feelout game. That isn't the time to break in new moves or to be a cowboy. There's no upside, and people will still fuck you up for a nickel. Maybe they'll fuck you up more for a nickel—it's a different class of person. If your bottom deal isn't perfect at home, don't practice it in a nickel-and-dime game for shits and grins. You could end up with plenty of shit and no grins. In a little game, even if they don't rough you up when they catch you, they definitely won't invite you to a bigger game. There are no "practice games." Fuck up alone in front of a mirror, just like you jerk off. All your moves have got to be automatic. Never get caught. It's worth repeating.

Even if you practice until your fingers bleed and you do everything in your power to keep from getting caught, it can still happen. One day there will be more than twenty large on the table and you're going to want it all. You're going to cheat and keep cheating until it's all yours. You'll mix it up, of course; you'll use different techniques and you'll spread it out. You won't go for the whole bundle on one impossibly lucky draw, but you don't want to spend all night cheating, either. You want to win as much in as few dirty hands as you can. But one night, they might get really lucky and catch you.

What happens when you get busted dead to rights? Nothing good. Let's deal with the worst-case scenario. How bad does it get? Worse than you think.

First, they'll block the exits. They'll get that idea as fast as you get the idea of running away. While you're still talking, working an alibi, they'll be trying to corner you like the rat that you are. If no one at the table has been cheated before, they may not get all the exits covered. Run like a motherfucker. If you run and get away, it should teach you to be more careful next time.

Guys who've been cheated before (by you or by anyone else) will jump into action quicker. They've spent plenty of time fantasizing about what they'd like to do to the guy who hustled them, and you've given those guys the chance live out their revenge fantasies. They'll be angry and ready.

You can't fight your way out, so don't try. It's the worst thing you can do. If a player starts pushing you or gets in your face, screaming, cussing out your mother . . . you play dumb. It doesn't matter how badly busted you are. If someone grabs your hand and six aces fall out of your sleeve, admit nothing. Those cards aren't yours. No fucking way! Swear to god. On your mother's eyes. What can you say? Act surprised. Some guy's walked in and caught you with his wife, your prick is up to the hilt in her asshole, and now you're going to look him dead in the eye and deny you ever met her. Say "Cheating????" like you have no fucking idea what the word even means.

If they keep yelling, you can yell back a little because you're mad and shocked that they'd accuse you of such a thing. If all they're doing is yelling, that's good. Keep them yelling. Don't make things worse. It'll only be one or two guys who will start a confrontation. Don't look those two in the eye much; just like a bear, that'll make them attack.

Don't try to be cute and smile and play the "aw shucks, you got me" card. The only time you can pretend the cheating was a joke is if you act fast enough that you're practically turning yourself in before someone gets to say, "Hey, he's doing something on the deal!" If

that happens, tell them you were trying a trick. Say you're a magician. Say anything. But let them know you're scared. That'll be
easy—you *will* be scared to death. Piss your slacks. Shit yourself.
Throw up. All of that is okay. Make yourself so disgusting that they
won't want to touch you. They have to touch you to hit you.

Try to find someone to be the voice of reason. "It's just a card
game, Jesus!" That's what you want to hear. Get someone reason-
able to calm everyone the fuck down. Look for a sympathetic face.
Try to spot a guy who won't look back at you. He's the guy who's
afraid to get involved. Suck him in. Ask him what's happening. Call
him by name. Deflect the anger on him. Say things like, "You never
told me this could happen!" and "This was your idea, Bub, help me
out!" Make it clear that he's your partner. Say, "I thought you said
these guys were easy money!" It's tough shit for that guy, but it may
buy you a little time when they turn their focus on him. If you can
make a break for it, take it. Use any distraction you can get and run.

When someone steps up to help you, don't hang them out to
dry. If someone tries to calm everyone down, do whatever he says.
Let him be the peacemaker. You want peace at all costs. Get everyone sitting down, and you can make the offer to call for law enforcement professionals to settle everything. The second you see a
chance, bolt for the door. Tip over as many chairs, lamps, pillows,
and anything else you can to slow down your pursuers.

If everyone is screaming at you and they're getting ready to
start hitting, you've got to try to cannonball: Cover your head with
your arms, duck down a little, and run as hard and fast as you can.
Remember, don't hit anyone. If your hands go near anyone, they'll
fucking kill you. If you bump or push them, that's okay, but don't
start any contact. No punching or kicking.

Whenever things look bad and you make a dash to get the hell
out, you might want to throw down some cash. Use your *Michigan*

bankroll. Keep it handy at all times. This is your roll of ones covered by a twenty, fifty, or hundred on the outside that you use to impress whores. Throw that money on the table. It looks like a lot more cash than it is. Say that you'll give them all of your money, then take out your roll, toss it away from you, and try to walk. If they go for the money, run for your life.

Always make sure you can get in and out of your car fast. Never get parked in. You don't want to park in the driveway of the home you'll be playing at. Park down the street, on the curb. If you're in the driveway it's harder to get out. You'll make enough money cheating to have a really nice car, but don't use that car to go to work. Drive an old clunker. Keep the keys in the ignition and all the doors except the driver's side locked. It's ready to go.

Don't worry about your car getting stolen. You'll be playing mostly in good neighborhoods. If your car does get pinched, it's a chance for a friend to help you out with a ride. It'll give you a good story, and sympathy from the other players for the next week. If your car happens to be stolen the same night that you get busted cheating, then god wants you dead and there's nothing you can do about it.

Even though the key is in the junker, you'll still have your Lexus (or whatever) keys on you. Use that as collateral to settle people down. Make sure you have keys to your hotel room in your getaway car's glove box. If they have your (fake) keys, they'll think you can't get away. Practice getting into your car, getting it started, and driving fast. You should be as good at getting your car moving fast as you are at palming seven cards.

You might get grabbed or hit. If you can't get away, you're going to take a beating. Getting beat up isn't the best part of the job, but if you know how to take it, you'll be better off. Cover your face.

They'll want to pry your arms away so they can bloody you up, but always protect your face. Don't fall to the ground right away . . . take a few shots standing up. Bend over a little and try to keep your balls tucked between your legs. Remember to keep screaming "please" and "no more." This isn't a good time to tell them all to fuck themselves; you were cheating and you got caught. Don't do anything to make them madder at you, and don't stop claiming you're innocent. Take a few good shots, then fall to the ground and curl up. Watch for kicks to the head. The back of the head is pretty sturdy, but if you get kicked in the nose, you'll be bleeding so much that you won't be able to see.

It takes a lot out of a man to beat another man senseless. That works in your favor. Even if there are eight of them, pushing and punching gets tiring fast. Eight guys won't fuck you up more than three guys because it's too crowded for everyone to hit at once. They have to take turns, and after a few licks from everyone, people will feel like you've had enough. Once you're on the ground, you can stop screaming because you want them to think that you're hurt too much to yell. You *will* be in bad shape, but you always want them to think that you're hurt worse than you are. You want them to worry. If there's blood, let them see it. Get as much blood on your clothes and on the floor as possible. Cower like a dog. Let them think they went too far. If they think you could die, that's great. That will get them to back off. They'll be relieved to see you run.

It's really hard to beat a man to death. You might get cut up badly and need to visit a hospital. You might have a few broken bones—there's a pretty good chance they'll want to stomp your hands to keep you from doing shifty moves ever again. Hand stompings hurt—a lot—but you'll live, and later you'll just have to learn the moves again with your new hands. You could get some cracked ribs or a concussion, and you might need stitches. You'll survive it. Even so, you really don't want to get caught.

Because you know you'll survive, you don't have to panic. Keep your head, stay in control, and keep looking for any way out. It's survivable. If someone pulls a knife, begging and running are more important. If there's a gun, begging is your first choice and you want to be as sure as you can be that you won't get shot in the back if you run. If you see knives or guns, it's not necessarily the worst thing in the world. Angry mobs are a little less likely to beat you because the knives and guns give them all the power, and no one wants to use a weapon. Still, call for help. Yell "fire!" Yell "police!" and try to hide behind other people. Keep pissing, shitting, and vomiting, and hope for pity and disgust.

You don't want to fight back because there's a good chance that someone will call the police (especially if there's a lot of screaming) before anything physical happens. You want law enforcement professionals to be there. They are your best friends. Home games are fun, but they're usually not legal (and this is one of the reasons why). Stick to your story if the law arrives. It's all a misunderstanding, but people started to threaten you. You'll be told never to come back (that'll be fine by you) and the host will be told it's too much of a hassle to press charges.

If the law doesn't show up until after you've been beaten up pretty good, you tell them that you were attacked by the other players and that you want to press charges. The chumps will keep screaming that you cheated them. You stick to your story: you have no idea what they're talking about, and you want them all in jail. The police won't want to haul everyone away, and they're unlikely to let you walk—they take everyone or no one to jail, usually. If you haven't thrown a punch, it's really hard for them to lock you up. If you're the one who's beat to shit and everyone else is okay, the law enforcement professionals will take your side (whether they want to or not). The other players might lie and say that you started a fight, but the truth is in the bruises. You might be forced to give back some of the money, but you won't get jail time. Prison home games aren't nearly as profitable.

Getting fucked up might also mean losing a big bankroll. That's why lesson number one is to Get The Money. If you have it on you, a group of angry players won't try to get the money first. They want blood. You can always make more blood. They won't be thinking about searching you for cash, so stash it and hope. If you feel like things are getting ugly, make a grab for the bank and explain that they're all trying to cheat you. Take as much as you can. If you can't get to the money before things get physical, you can always try coming back when you're healed up and threaten to sue if you don't get your money back. A little blackmail goes a long way. You worked hard for that money and you deserve it. You can even hire a lawyer. You'll have a police report, a guy who's running an illegal poker game out of his house, and a pile of doctor's bills . . . maybe they'll settle. Give it a try. I wouldn't make a career out of getting beaten for money, but play the cards you're dealt (for a change).

You can avoid most of these problems by carrying a gun. Don't use it to rob people; use it only for self-defense. With a gun on you, everything changes. It doesn't matter how many of them there are. If you pull a gun and someone else has a gun, they're not going to reach for it. You have the drop on them, and they won't want to upset the guy with the drawn gun.

I don't carry a gun. I can't really explain why. Maybe I don't trust myself. I can get mad and crazy. But if you're a real pro card cheat, a gun will take care of most of the problems discussed in this chapter. You still don't want to get caught. But if you are? Wave the gun around, walk to your car, and drive away forever.

Better yet, *don't get caught.*

· Chapter 26 ·

SLAMMING THE POT

You should always be trying to get the most money you can. Don't limit yourself; there's more than one way to skin a cat (although I can't think of even a single one). Keep all your options open. You always need to be ready to improvise. Use any opportunity to take advantage of your "friends."

Sometimes the fringe benefits are almost as good as the money itself (I said *almost*). You are likely to meet women in home games (both players and players' wives) and you can get decent pussy without it costing you a penny. If you are good at working people, women can help you make money, too.

More women play poker these days. It gives them a little power rush to win money off of a bunch of men. Guys don't like to invite ladies to play with them. Men want to be men, use foul language, smoke, and drink. Married men want to tell stories about their glory days of pussy hunting, and they can't do that with the ball and chain sitting next to them at the table telling them to ante up.

Once in a blue moon, you'll find some crusty old crow who knows the game and doesn't care about playing with the boys; she just wants to win. Her money is as good as anyone else's, but one old bat can scare away all of your pigeons. No one wants to lose to a woman.

Try not to be bothered by the women who play cards. I don't care at all. If there's enough money on the table, I don't care what the players have between their legs.

These days, it's not rare to see a game with couples playing together. The men are sensitive, caring . . . and totally emasculated. Their peckers are in their wives' designer handbags. Couples who play poker are mostly young and are playing because it's the "thing to do." Couples play for chump change, except in California and New York, where people in the jet set want to be part of the latest thing. More often than not, though, the man plays poker and the woman makes the snacks.

Wives are resentful of poker. It takes time, attention, and money away from them. If her husband is the host, the wife is the one who'll have to clean up and ask people not to get ashes on the rug. Guys will try to get their wives out of the house when they have a game. If the women stick around, the men will bark at their wives during the games to prove to their buddies who's wearing the pants. The poker wife has a tough time.

If you have an ounce of charm, the poker wife will adore you. You always bring a bottle of wine or a six-pack to every game, and if there's a cute wife, bring her some flowers, too. The husband won't say anything because it'll keep her off his back until after you leave. Wear a wedding ring and talk fondly about your wife during games. Don't give the host any reason to think you are trying to fuck his wife.

Make sure he doesn't get that idea, because, of course, you're going to fuck his wife. There are plenty of reasons to do this besides the sex. Once you've fucked a guy's wife, you've got even more leverage on him. If you have to blow town, you can let him know that she had an affair with you, and he'll be upset about you fucking her instead of thinking about you fucking him at the table.

You can use his wife against him. You can hint to her that you're feeling guilty and you might have to tell her husband. She won't want that to happen and you can use that pressure to get some extra money out of her if you promise to leave town. Once you're gone, she'll be really nice to him because she feels guilty about cheating on him. He'll be nice to her because he feels guilty about all the money he lost to you. You've made them a happier couple. You're spreading good will by spreading her legs. You're practically Cupid.

When you hear table talk from a suspicious husband that his wife might be cheating on him, it's a great time to start fucking his wife. Then, spread some nasty rumors about people screwing around on each other, and you can put the table on instant tilt. Everyone will be distracted and angry. Put players against each other. Tell one husband that you heard that one of the unmarried players had been seen around town with his wife. He won't be able to think about cards. You clean up and you get pussy. Neglected, resentful wives are good in bed, too. They want to prove to themselves that they're still sexy. You can help them with that.

You'll learn the tells for a bad marriage. Bad marriages are a lot more common than you might think. There's at least one at every table. Maybe poker attracts fucked-up people, or maybe poker fucks them up. What do you care? Whatever the reason, it's easy to get under the skirt of the average poker housewife.

You've got to be charming to make money at poker anyway, so use it on the housewife. Ask her about herself. Ask her about her life. Remember something she tells you one week, and bring it up the next week. Look her in the eye. Compliment her hair. Don't bring up sex, let her work it into the conversation. Once she opens that door, you walk right on in.

After a few poker sessions, "accidentally" swipe a hat or glove out of the closet when you leave the game. The next morning, when the husband's at work, stop by his house to return the hat or glove. Chat with the wife for a while. She'll invite you in for coffee. Talk about her husband. Ask her how things are going. The floodgates will burst open. If there are any problems between her and the old man, she'll get to talking. Be there for her. Hold her hand. Rub her back. Pretty soon, you'll be rubbing your face in her tits.

This book isn't about how to get laid, but cheating is cheating. Once you've got the wife cheating with you while you cheat the husband at cards, you've got a great way to keep him tilting like the fucking Tower of Pisa. Eventually, he'll figure out she's humping someone behind his back, and that will affect his card playing. If he suspects you, he'll play cards to fuck you (big aggressive bets) and it'll cost him. If the wife worries he's going to catch on, then you do a little light blackmail.

You've got nothing to worry about. If he's going to stand up and accuse you during a game, you'll smell it coming. It'll be written on his face. Bleed all the cash from the players as fast as possible, and when he accuses you, flat out deny it. Cash out, be offended, and tell him you'll talk about it after he calms down and apologizes. You'll be gone forever. You fucked his friends; you fucked his wife; you fucked him. *Trifecta.*

Men are more likely to get violent over you fucking their wives in their own bedrooms than they are to get violent over you cheating at cards. If you get cornered, don't try to pretend that you're a fairy. I saw a guy called Swifty try that at a game. He'd been porking the wife of Klink, our host. I know this because I'd tried to lay her, too, and I could tell that she had some secrets. Klink called Swifty out in the middle of a game, and Swifty (who was never married) said he was a queer. That didn't work for Swifty at all. They believed him, and he was beaten to a bloody pulp by everyone at the table for being a faggot, even while Klink's wife (that whore) begged for them to stop. It all worked out good for me, because they left all the money on the table. I took it, called the cops, and that was that.

It's hard to have a real relationship when you're always on the road making money. Take advantage of the loneliness that's all around you. She'll be happy, you'll be happy, and there'll be more in your wallet. Everybody wins.

· Chapter 27 ·
SHARKING

You can make a lot of money at the card table. Sometimes, though, you'll want to make more than the players have on the felt in front of them. Why not? If you're going to be a card shark, you might as well be a loan shark, too.

Most people plan how much they can lose at poker and you'll be taking that entire poke from them. They'll get pissed, but most of the time you're not winning someone's tough money. It's an entertainment expense that they can afford to lose, and they're getting more than their money's worth. I give them an exciting game. I teach them humility. I show them that they can't get something for nothing. And I make a good living.

When people lose more than they can afford, they might need a loan to buy food or pay the rent. You can help them out of a tight spot.

A real loan shark has to be willing to hurt people to get them to pay, and loan sharking will get you in more hot water with law enforcement professionals than playing in an illegal card game ever would. There are more laws to stop people from loaning each other money than there are laws to keep people from gambling. The banks have more muscle than the casinos, and they want all the action for themselves. Still, everybody does it, and there's lots of money to be made from lending. So why shouldn't you do it, Shylock?

The beautiful thing about poker is that players have good nights and bad nights (unless they're cheating), and since it's all for fun, they might find themselves coming up a little bit light. They're playing with friends, and a friend will always step up and loan them a few bucks to keep the good times rolling. When you loan someone money, you're being the generous good guy. Your friends will trust you more, and it puts more money on the table.

People who borrow money usually don't play well. They get self-conscious. A little internal voice is screaming at them, "Don't fuck this up, asshole! Loser!" They know they've lost more than they should have at one game, and that gets them to make mistakes. And that's good for you. You take a guy for a few hundred bucks, loan him a few hundred more, and take that off of him, too. Then, on top of everything else, he owes you.

You're not going to collect any juice and you're not going to go around breaking legs to get your money back, but loaning money is a good way to launder some of your winnings. You can use loans to hide how much you're winning. Once you've stuck one player for all he's worth and loan him more, any winnings he makes will go right back to you to pay off his debt. Yet the other players at the table will remember that he won those hands. This is one of those lessons that I can't repeat enough: It's always better to have other players think that you're not the only one at the table who's winning.

Give your borrower winning cards until you get your money back; if anyone suspects cheating, they'll think he's the one doing it. You've made a partner who can't sell you out and who you don't have to share with. Give a guy a grand to keep playing. If his luck changes and he starts to win? That's money that you don't have to be seen winning from another player. Spread the wealth.

A loser who's loaned money will stay in the game longer and that's good for you one way or another. When you become the bank, you're being the nice guy that everyone knows you are; you're giving a break to a guy who hit a streak of bad luck. You're the big winner in the games you play in, and you want people to think that winners are nice guys who don't care much about money. You build up the idea that all good winners should loan money to friends who've had a bad beat. This helps set up other players to loan money to each other, too.

Maybe one day you want to set up your game so that you're not the big winner. Maybe you see to it that a couple of guys get cleaned out completely. Someone's got to loan them money to keep the game going. Now keep in mind that I'm not talking about scooting or horsing; these are table stakes games, and you're not allowed to pass chips between players. That's a rule you'll follow. You don't want to sneak them chips, you want to loan them money. You're bringing more money into the game. If anyone tries to pass some of their chips to someone else, you should point out that it's against the rules (and it is). Sharing chips is a kind of collusion and that's cheating, and we all know that cheating is wrong.

So, the big winner at the game has to dig into his pocket and bring more real money into the game to keep the losers playing. After the losers are both in debt, you stick everyone for heavy losses. The winner winds up losing the most, and you won't be the one that has debts to collect—he will. You'll leave with more cash than the game was worth.

You want players loaning money to each other as often as possible. More money loaned is more money on the table. It gets players to dip into their tough money. It's money they might not have had any intention of gambling themselves, but they can loan it to a friend because they know it will get paid back. He's good for it. He probably is, but what the fuck do you care? You have the cash.

Say you've got a six-handed game. Each player buys in for a grand. That's five grand you can take from the table (you don't count the money you're bringing to the table). If you arrange for three people to bust out early, you might get the other two people to give the three losers $200 extra each. You now have the total on the table up to $5,600. That adds up fast.

When you're the banker, don't loan money out too easily because people will be suspicious. Don't be the only generous one; encourage other people to start loaning money, too. Once in a while, refuse to do it; claim you're a little short that week. Make up a bullshit story about losing a big golf bet and ask someone else to lend the other player the money. The more people who loan money, the better for you.

Keep in mind that the players you loan extra cash to will sometimes end up resenting you. Especially if (when) they lose. They will have gone from playing for fun, to getting cleaned out, to getting cleaned out *and* owing another guy money. They might think that owing someone money from a stupid game is different than a car payment. Some people think losing money at cards can still be fun; no one thinks that paying off a debt is fun.

Always take checks from other players. If they're borrowing money, they won't have cash, so what else would they do? Give you an I.O.U.? Fuck that. Just tell them to give you a check. If they try to play the "You know I'm good for it" bullshit, you laugh and smile and pat them on the back and say "Sure!" Then ask them for a check in front of the other players. Be friendly, but shame them into giving you bank paper.

Sometimes a player will ask you to hold on to his personal check and not cash it until a later date. You should always agree to that and then be sure you cash that check the very next business day. When you lower his bank balance, he might borrow money from other players to get by. If he gets mad that you cashed the check before you said you would, tell him the wife deposited it by mistake. If the check bounces, the bank can shake him down. You want to leave the collecting to the pros.

You never know what kind of dishonorable scumbag a person is until you loan him money. You'll get welchers. They might want to try to win back their debts, and you have to put the kibosh on that immediately. If someone owes you anything one week, you need to get paid before you'll play with that person again. There's no use cheating to win promises. Let them borrow from another player to pay you back, but you want your debt settled up right away. Once bitten, twice shy. Don't make too big of a stink about it, but you need to put pressure on a borrower's other friends so you can leave with cash. If he doesn't have cash, maybe he has a gambling problem and needs to be cut off.

If your marker is still not paid off, it may be because the lowlife knows that you can't force him to pay. It's not a legally recognized loan. It's not usury because there's no juice, but still, it's hard to get the law involved. That's okay. Once you've burned the game, show up at his job and ask about the money. Start calling his wife and friends. With that kind of pressure, almost everyone will pay up. You'll never be able to play poker with him again, but who cares? You got the cash.

Don't worry, though, most people are good for it. Honest working men take their debts seriously. There are people with gambling problems who seek out home games (go figure) and you'll know if you're going to get paid back within a week. If not, end the gravy train and get someone else to loan the chump some change. You can't waste your time collecting markers.

Setting yourself up as a nice guy who'll loan money to other players will pay off again when you're ready to burn a game. Make sure all of the debts owed to you are paid in full and then hit a little bit of bad luck yourself. You can borrow anywhere from a few hundred to a few thousand to keep playing. Since you're one of the consistent winners in the game, you'll be able to get a bigger loan than anyone else. Be sheepish and embarrassed about not bringing more money to the game.

Once you've borrowed some money, pull out the stops and clean everyone out as quickly as possible. It'd be best to win a lot on a hand that's a bad beat for another guy. While everyone's talking about it, collect your money and haul ass. Nowadays I make my cell phone ring. I have a fake fight with my wife and act like I just got told my kid is in the hospital. Tell everyone you'll see them next week, and head to your car. The guy who loaned you money won't have a chance to ask to get paid back because at first, you were celebrating and excited about your lucky win, and then you were in a panicked rush to get to the hospital. What kind of fucking asshole would ask you for a payback when your kid is vomiting blood in the emergency room? Everyone assumes you'll be back the next week, you're the only one who knows that you're gone forever. For all they know your fucking kid died and you stuck your head in an oven. You keep all the winnings on top of the loans. No one is going to cause trouble where you work or harass your friends now, are they?

After I made the Big Mistake, I turned my back on cards for a while and tried to get by on loan sharking. That was a nifty trick since I didn't have a goddamned dime to my name, but I've got a nice face and people like me. I borrowed half a yard from a friend and used it to make a loan to a heavy dice player I knew. I got a lot of juice on that deal—the craps guy got lucky for a change—and I had a fifty percent return on my money in a week. I did that for a while, getting markers from gamblers, drug addicts, and hookers, but it's a tough way to make a living. I was only loaning small amounts, and it was always friendly, but it's nerve-wracking. Junkies can be crazy, and they'll spend any money they get on more junk instead of paying off loans. Whores can always get money, but you have to be there when they've got it in order to get it back. I worked that racket for three months, got a new bankroll, and went back to cheating. It's what I do best.

It doesn't suit me, but if there's any profession that comes close to cheating at poker for high profit and easy work, it's got to be banking. We Jews have the right idea. *Mazel tov.*

Chapter 28

NUTS

Poker players love nuts. They like to eat nuts while they're drinking their beer. They've got to be nuts to stay in some hands. They've got to have big hairy nuts to risk it all at the table. You've got them by the nuts whenever you're in a game.

Every player wants the nuts: the best hand possible. If you're playing draw poker and your first five cards are the 10–J–Q–K–A of spades, you won't be drawing because your hand can't get any better. It's time for a big bet. You got the nuts.

In Hold 'Em, you won't always know what the absolute nuts are until the river. If you get a flop with 8–8–3 and you're sitting on a pair of 8s, you can still be beat. It's unlikely, but it's still a beatable hand. What if the turn and river are both kings and the slob next to you has a pair of kings in the hole? Sure, you won't let that happen, but it's important to think about the nuts when you're setting up your cheating strategy.

A lot of times, people will think that they've got an unbeatable hand. You want them to forget that four 8s can be beaten by four kings. Be very careful when you beat a powerhouse hand with another powerhouse hand, because even to a simpleton it looks like a setup. You don't want to beat four of a kind with a higher four of a kind; you want to out-kick your opponent.

I was heads-up with Chunky in a No Limit game with a joker (yup, losers love their wild cards, so get used to it). I gave Chunky K–8 of diamonds in the hole. He brought it in for two hundred bucks because heads-up that's a fine hand (and he was a good enough player to know it was a fine hand. You have to cheat to the level of your opponent). The flop came 3–K–8. I made a medium bet, and Chunky called me. Fourth street was another king. I checked; Chunky bet heavy into me. At this point, he had a full house, kings over eights. It wasn't the nut hand, but it was rock solid. We each had about half our chips in the pot. The river brought the wild card, and when he saw it, he practically jumped out of his seat. That gave him four kings!

I made a bet too small for the size of the pot, and Chunky raised me. He didn't raise me everything because he didn't want to scare me away. I re-raised him a little bit more, and he re-reraised me all-in. He was so happy. He got everything into the pot on four kings. His big fat smile faded away when I turned over my K–10. I also had four kings, but my ten kicker was higher than his eight. Amazing how the cards fall, isn't it?

Chunky was a good enough player that he should've known his hand was beatable. He went from a full house to four of a kind and, in the excitement, he stopped paying attention to the fact that three of his four kings were in the window, which meant I got to use them, too. His kicker seemed real good at the start of the hand when he had top two pair, but he forgot that with a wild card it's possible to have more than four of a kind. My betting made sense to him be-cause it looked like I was slow-playing my own four of a kind, and he beat himself up for being so stupid. I want them to beat them-selves up. I just don't want them beating me up. It was close enough to a win that he hated himself, and so close to a win that he wanted to play again. That's the way it should work.

For whatever reason, a lot of guys think that a straight is a nut hand. If you play thousands of hands of poker, you notice that most big pots are taken down with two pair or three of a kind. Straights and higher aren't rare, but they're usually good enough for a win. I like to give a guy a straight on the flop. He'll push it hard all the way to the river. Two hearts on the flop, a third on the river, and I turn over my two high hearts at the showdown. He'll never even think that someone had a flush draw because he was so eager to pump up that pot for his bullshit straight.

Another favorite move of mine is to beat a flush with a full house. In a medium-stakes game, I gave three people pocket spades. In the cut-off seat, Chip got A–10 of spades. When the flop came Q–J–4 of spades, Chip almost fell out of his seat. He had the nut flush and a draw on a royal flush! There was a lot of action; the other two guys with pocket spades had lesser flushes (one was king-high, the other was nine-high). I kept up with them. The turn showed a jack of diamonds, and fifth street was a two of spades. The king-high flush stayed with Chip all the way, and so did I. Chip was sure he won. When I showed my jacks full of queens, Chip practically shit himself. It's one of the best stacks you can use. You can't do it often, because it's too unlikely to happen more than once, but at the exact right time of the night, you'll make a bundle. I use the same stack in most burn games. They get a once-in-a-lifetime story; you tell the same story again and again. The chumps change, the cards and the hero stay the same.

People have a really tough time laying down good cards. It happens to everyone. It gets harder when the hand is bigger. With a wild card in play, people forget that the best hand isn't a royal flush . . . it's five of a kind. Players who get a monster hand usually get distracted—they're excited but don't want to show it, so they focus on looking calm. They think about winning the pot, they think about getting the biggest payback they can. They don't always stop and think about whether they can still be beaten, and those are all good things.

The nuts have many names. The Brass Brazilians. Holy City. Chingaderos. Golyoonies. Iron Duke. Honeymoon in Bali. Jerusalem. Immortal. Whatever the fuck you want to call them, the nuts are your friend when one of your players thinks he's got them. Then you put his real nuts in a vice . . . and squeeze.

Chapter 29

LIVE AND LEARN

Okay, here's the best tip in the book. I'm going to tell you the granddaddy of all fuckups, and I know it well because I'm the one who made it. I didn't make it early in my career, either. I wasn't a stupid kid who didn't know any better. I made the Big Mistake when I *did* know better. It cost me everything that was important in my life, and it almost cost me my life, too . . . but who would've fucking cared at that point?

I didn't have a book telling me how to cheat. I was on my own. I read books about the moves and I learned them. I'd hang around card rooms and watch for hours, never playing a hand. I'd listen to old-timers tell stories. Then I'd play poker. Thousands, probably millions of hands (okay, probably hundreds of thousands—it's good that you're paying attention). I'd been cheating since my first nail nick on that old ace of hearts, and I never gave another thought to playing a game without cheating. I would hardly play a hand unless I had some kind of advantage on it: maybe I'd be marking a card or putting in a crimp, or maybe I'd sneak a peek or cop chips. I worked on my skills every chance I got, and every deal of the cards was another chance. You do something *millions* of times (including practice), you'll get good at it, too.

You never want to let your guard down because that's when

you get punched in the face. You never want to think that you know it all. You never want to think you're the best in the world. You might be the best in the world, but who gives a rat's ass? In this line of work, being the best means nothing, because no one can ever know. You'll never know until card cheating becomes an Olympic sport, and then you'll be beaten by some barefoot African on steroids. Whenever you start to think you can't be cheated, you'll be cheated. Whenever you think you're so good you can't get busted on a move, you'll get busted on a move. There's no reason to be humble—you've just got to realize that pride will set you up for a hard fall.

Disaster will hit you. That's part of this game, too. Disaster will hit even if you don't fuck up because even when you're cheating, you're still gambling, and gambling always has some risks (that's why they call it "gambling"). Maybe you won't get paid. Maybe you'll get accused of cheating when you didn't. Maybe some crooks will bust into your game and rob you at gunpoint. Maybe a guy you've played with for years will get sore at a bad beat one day and bloody your nose.

All this is true, but I'm just avoiding getting into the lesson I learned from the Big Mistake. It pisses me off just to think about it. It crippled me. I came real close to jumping off a fucking bridge. You ever have something happen to you that's so bad that after it you can't imagine living? It was worse than that.

It was my own fault. I fucked up. If you do something so stupid that it costs you all you have, and you can't do anything about it, then everything gets difficult. It even gets hard to breathe. I've been playing cards without a problem for almost as long as I've been breathing, so maybe I'd fuck up breathing, too.

If a tornado blows down your house and destroys everything you love? That's too bad, but you'll get over it. Those things happen. Move on. But if you're smoking in bed and you burn down your house with your wife, your kids, and your dog? You've got to live

with the fact that you killed them. It was your smoking. Your stu-
pidity. Your carelessness. How do you go on with your life after
that? Who's going to forgive you? God? Fuck that. Why would god
let your family roast in the first place?

In my line of work, I confide in no one. *No one.* This book is it.
I don't have friends, and I wouldn't talk to them if I did. I don't tell
my stories to the women I screw. I keep it all inside, where it be-
longs. It might have been nice to sit down with a shrink, spill my
guts, and get rid of some of the pain sitting on my chest, but I know
what he'd say to me. There's only one thing *to* say—"You fucked up,
you fucking loser asshole." I already know that.

I didn't make the decision to burn that big game with Judge
and the rest of the seven-figure-income gang in New Hampshire. I
lost control. It was the apple of all apples, it made me a lot of
money, and I fucked it up.

I was in New Hampshire for the big game and I met a woman.
She was a whore, but not the kind you usually see in big cities. She
didn't just fuck for money. She really got off on getting strangers
off, so she was a great lay. I rented her for a few hours when I first
got to town. I didn't know she was a working girl when I first saw
her; she was dressed like a woman about to paint her bathroom. I
chatted her up at a bar and I was a bit surprised when she told me
her price. What did I care? A couple of hundred off my bankroll for
the next day's game wouldn't even make a scratch. I always like to
go into big games feeling relaxed, so she was a business expense.

We spent a full day together. Her lips were flapping every second that they weren't wrapped around my prick. She told me her
whole life story . . . it wasn't the bullshit sob story you usually get
from women. She was happy. She enjoyed her life. She didn't feel
guilty or ashamed. She didn't have any delusions about what she
was. She didn't tell herself she was sucking cock to make money for

law school; she'd grown up in a family with a lot of money. They loved her and would have given her as much money as she wanted with no questions or catches. She didn't whore because she had to; she did it because she wanted to. She wanted to make it on her own.

She was also a tight young piece of ass. We fucked until I could barely walk (she could walk fine—the slut), and then I gave her a ride back into town. She gave me half of her price back. She said she had a great time. It must be like dumping the last hand of the evening to make everyone at the table want to come back for more. And you know what? It works.

The local sheriff rolled by as she was getting out of my car. She saw him and turned away. It was a small enough town that the sheriff knew all the troublemakers and lawbreakers (except for me). He cherry-topped and tapped the siren and rolled over to us. He pulled her over to his car and asked her some questions. After a few minutes, he loaded her into the cruiser, then he came up to me and said she was a known prostitute. No shit.

I smiled and told the law enforcement professional I was just giving her a lift (I gave her a lift, all right). I explained that I was in town to see Judge, and that shut him the fuck up. He drove off with her, and she waved at me from the back of his cruiser and smiled. A class act.

The big game was that night. I remember every fucking detail. It was a cool night, and I got there about twenty minutes later than everyone else. I had the biggest bankroll I've ever had on me. I even worried about getting mugged—what if some two-bit asshole with a gun tried to roll me? Would I fight back? None of that would happen. I was in New Hampshire, for christ's sake, on my way to a judge's house. But if I did get robbed, my talk with the sheriff would come back and bite me on the ass.

I cleared my head and walked into the house. For this game, I had bought an expensive suit (which I had dry-cleaned twenty times in a row to make it look like I'd worn it before). I aired it out but it still smelled like cleaning chemicals. I knew the cigar smoke would cover that. The suit was loaded for work with three cold decks.

My bankroll was big. It was big for me, and it was big for any-one. Five million. What the fuck? Yeah, that's right. I had five mil-lion on me: $100,000 in cash (why the fuck don't they have bills bigger than hundreds?) and a cashier's check for the rest. I was the guy who convinced everyone in the game that we should deal in cash. (Cashier's checks *are* cash.) They used to play for smaller stakes (one-to five-thousand-dollar blinds), and I had pushed them up over the previous couple years. They had the money, they didn't care, but they played the "gentleman's game." Everyone knew every-one else was good for their debts. I pushed for cash. "It's more ex-citing," I told them. "There's a different feeling when you walk out of a game with a briefcase full of cash." No one fought me on it; they liked the idea. Rich people like the idea of rolling around naked in big piles of cash as much as poor people do.

I had worked my whole life to build my bankroll, and this was most of it. We'd bumped up the blinds over the last several games, and now we were playing $50,000/$100,000 blinds. Five mil would be the amount everyone would have for this game. That meant I'd have a shot at twenty-five million dollars. That's a big game for any-one. I was a little bit nervous about that much money. After that game, I was going to pull back a little bit. This was the score I needed to put my feet up. I could live very comfortably forever on that much money. Sure, I could've lived all right on five million bucks—it's not chicken scratch—but twenty-five million is better.

We played with chips, but this time each chip was fifty large. No chip copping in that game. People played tight, and I worked it easy for the first couple of hours.

At about 11 P.M., there was a knock at the door. Guess who came to dinner? The sheriff. He knew about the game, and he wanted to see what that much money looked like. He had his gun holstered on his hip, and I got a cold chill when he walked in the door. How much does a sheriff pull down in a year? He could've put a bullet in each of our foreheads and retired to the Bahamas. That was a lot of cash.

The sheriff wanted to make small talk with Judge, but with several million at stake in each hand, no one in the game was feeling chatty. The sheriff pulled up a chair and sat down to watch. He caught my eye and waved and smiled, and I waved and smiled back. I don't like guns being anywhere around me. I was paranoid; this was New Hampshire. They probably didn't even know that there was such a thing as a crooked cop. Maybe having him around would be good, I thought.

It was my deal (I had convinced them it was more fun without a pro dealer) and I switched in my ice. That stack doubled me up fast. It got even more action than I planned, and after my deal I was up to $11.5 million. This game had been worth all the work. I was happy as a pig in shit. I didn't know it, but I was headed for deep shit.

I fucked up. This wasn't the Big Mistake—it was just one of the little fuckups that happen during a game. I misread one of my marks or forgot something. I never misread my marks and I never forget anything, but whatever. I lost a hand that I didn't plan on losing. Maybe I was distracted because my bankroll had doubled a few minutes before. I don't know. I do know that Judge won thanks to my fuckup, and he was very happy to take two million dollars off of me.

Jesus fucking christ. It's *okay* to dump a hand to a guy. I'd dumped hundreds of thousands of dollars to Judge over the last year just to keep him interested. I would've dumped a big pot to him *sometime* that night, but I didn't mean to do it then. He was happy. He thought he outplayed me, and he started to brag a little. Cocksucker. I had to sit and smile and be gracious. I had to be happy about it.

And then I made the Big Mistake. My life changed. I would never be the same.

He got to me.

What am I going to do? Stand up and say, "You didn't outplay me, you fucking blowhard idiot, I forgot what hand you were dealt! I know every hand you're dealt. I decide when you win and lose. I'm running this fucking show. I know every card you'll get before you get it. I know every move you make because you do everything exactly the way I want you to do it. I am fucking God at this table, you asshole. I've taken you every time we've sat at the table, so shut your hole." No, I don't get to do that. I don't get to do anything but take their money and keep quiet about it.

My little mistake had cost me two million dollars. Those kinds of mistakes happen. No one was wise to what was going on, so it wasn't a big deal. It wasn't a big deal . . . until I made it a big deal.

Why I did what I did, I have no idea. Not a clue. Believe me, I've played it over and over and over again in my head, and I don't understand it. Pride? Anger? Tilt? I don't know. I never felt any of those things at the card table—ever. But I knew what I wanted to do, and I did it.

The Big Mistake. I decided to play him straight for one hand. I knew the game and the players; I didn't *have* to cheat to take his money. What the fuck? What the fucking fuck? Maybe the sheriff sitting there made me think twice about cheating? I know that's not true. He was a hick; he didn't even know my moves existed. I wasn't on tilt, either. I planned on dumping that much money over the next few hands anyway. I must have had something to prove to myself. Fuck me.

There's never a reason—*ever*—to play straight with another person. There has to be control to win every time, and cheating is the control. If you can beat a player every single time by playing fair, there's still no reason to risk it. The best player in the world can play the worst player in the world and, once in a while, the worst player in the world will win. It'll be much less than 50 percent of the time, but if you're risking your own money, you want a 100 percent guarantee of winning. Why would you ever take a chance on fair play? Why would I fucking do that?

You know what happened. We played the next hand. I didn't deal it, I had no stack in play, and I looked only at my own cards. I was dealt one of the weakest hands, and because I know so much about fucking poker, I decided to bluff the pot. I scared everyone out except for Judge, of course. The pot got up to several million and change; he kept me honest (in every sense) and I lost.

Then, Judge did something smart. He pushed most of his chips to one side, and he sat behind a log for the rest of the evening. The chips he pushed aside were chips he wouldn't bet on any hand, no matter what. He played with a small percentage of his profits. He didn't want to win twenty-five million, he was happy just to take more than eight million off of me. Very happy. Smug, even. Bastard.

I went back to cheating, but Judge wouldn't touch his profits. I'd seen it before. He'd be willing to lose a few hundred grand more, but he'd sit and watch so he could make it through the night as the big winner. I took another million off of the other players, but I was still down. At least the idea of getting ballsy and trying to clean out everyone right away never entered my pea brain. I knew I'd finish the night with a big fucking hunk taken out of my bankroll, but I had to eat it. The other players got scared when they saw me lose a lot (even to them) and they tightened up like that little whore's asshole. Judge wasn't playing. The game went on, but there weren't any big hands. I lost money. I lost my own money.

I got up. I was a good loser. A loser. I lost and I didn't plan to. What for? For being a fucking prick idiot. I'd lose a little bit of money in small games to get people to raise the stakes or to get invited to juicier games, but I never lost enough to notice. I noticed this. I had the chance to make up to twenty-five million dollars, and I lost 2.3 million by the end of the night. All my own doing. Nothing could have been worse. I'd rather the cop had shot me in the groin, taken every cent, and left me to die slowly and painfully. At least that wouldn't have been my own goddamn fault.

The worst part was that it killed my biggest game. Judge was happy. He was done. He'd gotten his big poker thrill, he enjoyed it, and he was done. He was the kind of guy that would've lost five million and come back and tried it again. But once he won, he was done. He'd beaten the best player he knew. He'd still play poker, but never at those stakes again. The other players were also scared off by the big payouts. Winning several million bucks in one night was a fantasy for them, until they saw someone *lose* that much and realized that it could have been them. But instead, it was me. Fuck me.

There was no point in going back to the game for ten or twenty thousand. I could have made back my losses, but I couldn't even stand the thought of being back at that table. I couldn't look at them. I didn't trust that I wouldn't go batshit, so I could never go back. I've never been back to New Hampshire. I can't even talk to anyone from Vermont because it's too close to that memory.

I couldn't look at myself in the mirror for weeks. I still feel sick about it. Honor and equal play on equal footing, being beaten fair and square; that's not worth 2.3 million dollars. That's only worth a lifetime of pain. Cheating every chance I got was worth more than five million. If there's a lesson to be learned, it's that you should never ease up, and don't even *think* about playing fair.

Before I left town, I found my cute whore and gave her five thousand to fuck me bareback. Then I told her to do whatever she had to do to get her pussy around Judge's little shriveled pecker. I had a drip and I wanted him to get it. She agreed to pass along my VD regards to Judge. A quick shot would take care of the syph, but the herpes would stay with him. The judge would have some explaining to do when his wife came down with it (if he even bothered fucking her anymore). I don't know if the hooker got him, but it makes me feel a little bit better to think that his Johnson will be itching under his robes for a good long while.

Chapter 30

SHILLING

Poker rooms use *shills* to beef up the action and make sure the tables stay full. The shills pretend to be playing for fun, but the house is paying them to keep the other players in the game.

The information in this chapter won't make you rich, but an opportunity is an opportunity. If you get lucky, this scam will get you some action and money when you can't find a game. Some men won't take money from a broad. If that's you, I respect that, but you might want to read this anyway because the principle is good, and I invented it. You won't see it anywhere else.

I travel. A lot. I live on the road dragging my ass from one game to another. I've spent more of my life behind the wheel than inside a woman's snatch if you total up all the hours. That's just a waste of life.

No matter how much you work, there's a lot of downtime in our business. Whenever I get to a new city, I spend a couple of days looking for action. I go to the usual hangouts, talk to people, and sniff around. If I find some good lobsters, it still might be several days before a game comes together. There's a lot of free time, even for a man of leisure.

If the town has one, I go to a titty bar. I like them. It's a great place to find games. Strip clubs are good for business, but even if poker players never set foot inside one, I'd still go. Women get naked and push their goods in your face for a couple of bucks. For a few more dollars, they'll really take care of you. What could be better than that?

I'm going to tell you.

I've got a way with people. Men want me to be their buddy. They don't know what it is about me, but I'm the kind of guy that they want to introduce as their pal. That's part of my job. Women think I'm charming. They don't all want to fuck me, but with a little work I can get most of the ones I want. Strippers always want to talk to me. I listen. I care about what they say—as far as they know. When I chat up a stripper, she doesn't think I'm just trying to get in her twat; I make her think I'm a nice man who's looking out for her.

I find a stripper that I like, usually one with big fucking heavers, and I call her over. I pay for a dance, and I look her in the eyes and talk to her the whole time. She'll tell me how she's only doing this while she's in school, or to support her little bastard at home, and I'll smile and nod like I care. Before the night is over, I'll tell her that I made a lot of money as a shill in dance clubs. I'll tell her I used to own a club in a big city (as far away as possible from where I am, like Vegas—the trim capital of the free world), and that since I sold it, I kind of miss the business. I'll tell her I helped promote dancers (they like to be called dancers), and that I still like to help a girl out once in a while.

They've never heard of a Titty Shill (there is no such thing), but they always believe me. That's my gift. When they're on the hook, I'll give them the pitch: I'll come in during a busy Friday or Saturday night. I'll find the guys with the most money, introduce myself, and join them. (I'm doing all the stripper's shopping for her. I'm seeing where all the money is and getting to know the guys.) When I have the right group of guys, I'll call her over for a lap dance.

She'll give me the hottest fucking leg hump anyone's ever seen. After the dance, I'll tip her $100, and make it clear that that's the right way to handle a dancer. I'll tell her it gets the other guys to spend much more money on her. I'll tell the boys how hot the dance was, how it was worth every penny, the whole nine yards. I'll do her selling so all she has to do is take it off and wiggle.

I'll tell the dancer that it'll work for her and she'll make 500 percent more. She won't even fucking know how much 500 percent more is, all she'll hear is the word "more." She'll know I have a way with people, and I'll make it clear that I can get horny guys to crack open their wallets and give her some green. She's smart and knows the business (yeah, sure . . . she has big tits; that *is* the business). I'll tell her that if she gives me 10 percent on every dollar over her average nightly take, I'll help her out.

Don't offer to help anyone for nothing. No one trusts that shit. No one does anything for nothing. I get nothing from her nightly take, just 10 percent over that. That's a great deal. That's a small percentage. She'll think about it for a while (it takes strippers a while, be patient), but sometimes she'll agree. I don't give a fuck; it's not my meal ticket. I'm off the clock, just looking at her tits and passing time. She doesn't have to say yes.

If she bites (I like when they bite), I ask her what she usually makes on a Friday. She'll always lie right to your face. She'll usually say a thousand bucks. Make it clear to her: The first grand is hers, and then anything over that, you'll take 10 percent. It's a great deal. In the real world, she probably makes two hundred flapping her tits, but you don't care. She's trying to scam you, even though you're trying to help her make big money.

I worked this deal with a pretty young piece of ass that grew up in Philadelphia. She wanted to be a nurse some day. Her name was—a stripper name—let's call her Candy, for all I care. They all use the same four names, anyway. Candy liked my idea, she thought it was "brilliant" (like she would know), and she told me to be there at eleven the next night. I told Candy to leave four $100 bills for my seed money with the bouncer at the front. "You'll be getting your own money back, and I'll pay the cut to the house out of my share when we split."

Candy had some brains to go with her knockers; she wasn't keen on seeding with her own money. I gave her a look that said, "How can you not know this shit?" I told her that I'd be tipping her with her own money, that's how it works. That leads to more tips for her; five times her normal take. She said she'd leave the money for me. She was ready; I don't think she ever figured out the math, but she trusted me.

I walked into the club on Friday, the bouncer slipped me four C-notes, and I got to the stage. I saw Candy in a nurse's outfit (she probably wrote it off her taxes for nursing school expenses), and I sat down next to a group that was there for a bachelor party. I thought long and hard about working on them for a card game, but they were all deep in the bottle and too young to have any serious gambling money. They did have serious pussy money, though.

I called Candy over and she gave me the hottest groin grind I've ever had. I mean, there isn't a state in this fine country where what she did was legal in public. In her line of work, hanging a bottom is a good thing. She finished me off and I openly put the $100 bill into her g-string, squeezed her tits, slapped her ass, and talked her up to the guys as she walked away. "You get what you pay for." "Now she likes this table." "You get much less than that for $500 from the rest of these skanks." "Those tits are real."

I got up after a while, caught Candy's eye, shot her a wink, and left the club. I kept the other three hundred she gave me. Maybe she got enough in extra tips to cover the money I left with, what the fuck do I care? I gave her the hundred dollars for the lap dance when I could've kept it all, and that was generous. I liked her.

It probably took her all night to figure out that I wasn't coming back. She must have gone up to the bouncer, crying, and he probably rolled his eyes at her and told her that she should spend more money on brains and less on implants. She might have offered to suck him off if he went after me. If he'd taken that deal, everyone would have been happy . . . pretty much.

Minus the cost of the first dance I got, I cleared $280, plus two lap dances from a girl who was trying to be hot, rather than going through the motions. It worked out well. It's not cheating at cards, but it worked. It's a good scam and I invented it. I only went all the way with it once, though.

I liked Candy (I must have a sweet tooth) and I thought about that great lap dance a lot after that. I still think about her. She liked me. We got along well. Less than a year later I was driving through the area, only a couple of hours away, so I took a detour to go back to her club. I thought I'd give her some of that money back since, if it wasn't for her, I never would have come up with the Titty Shill idea. I wanted to ask her to go out, and maybe fuck her (the good way this time). I asked around the club, but she was long gone. A dancer who knew her said she thought Candy was a nurse somewhere now.

Chapter 31

CHEATING IN THE TWENTY-FIRST CENTURY

T imes have changed. It used to be hard work to find good poker games in each city. That was most of the job. Now, poker is so popular that you can get onto a computer and find home games anywhere in the world.

People are so fucking stupid. There are people you can meet over the computer who have never seen you before, and they will invite you to come into their home and play with their friends for real money. I had a friend tip me off to this, and I still can't believe anyone would do it. Do they walk through Times Square with a bullhorn announcing, "I sure hate walking down these streets at night with all this cash on me!" I would expect a gang with guns to show up at their little house party and clean everyone out. It must happen—do you really want to make it public knowledge that you're hosting a $500-per-person buy-in? That's a lot of cash on the table. Then again, most people *are* honest. That's my bread and butter.

Here's another modern miracle: Checks clear a lot faster nowadays. You can deposit a check and have the money available instantly. That's great. You don't want to have to wait for a week while an out-of-town check clears. You want the cash quick; when you've got it, cancel the account.

Can we have a few cheers for the ATM? This contraption must have been created by a card cheat. In the old days, when people lost all their cash, that was it. The well was dry. Now, it's a five-minute drive and they come back with another few hundred. If they lose that, they can go back and take out more money against their credit cards. What could be better? It's so easy, it ought to be illegal.

Television is full of poker these days, and that gets more people wanting to play in live games. Why not? It sure looks easy to win. A bunch of professional poker players are being treated like fucking celebrities, too. They wear stupid hats and have nicknames. There was a time when being known as a pro was a bad thing because you couldn't get a game. Now, if you're on TV, people will piss themselves to lose their money to you.

If you ever get the chance to play with a pro in a home game, jump at it. The pros are the easiest money around. They make the right decisions all the time, and you'll get the most out of your cold deck work. Beginners won't always know that a hand is a heavy favorite to win, and they'll pussy out on you. The pros will be more aggressive and they aren't afraid to lose money. It's part of their job, and that will help you with your job. The other great thing about playing with pros is that there will *never* be any attention on you with a pro in the game. Everyone at the table will be watching the pro. Oh, look at him. See how he studies his opponents? See how he covers his cards? Look at the way he shuffles his chips. Pros know about cheating, but they don't see much of it in the games they play in. They're above it, and they don't look for it.

Be careful about nail marking with pros. Andy Fucking Bloch calls for a new deck every time someone farts near the cards. Some pros look for accidental nicks and stains and use them as honest readers, and that's no good for you. Stick with hold-outs and seconds and you'll do fine with the pros.

Believe me, some pros are ridiculously easy pickings. Cocky, too, and the rest of the table will enjoy seeing you (or anyone else) taking them down a notch. I did my part to make poker exciting and popular nationally; I deserve some of their money, anyway.

Poker is so popular these days that pros are doing "seminars" that you can pay a few hundred or a few thousand clams to sit in on. You can hear them talk about strategy and listen to their bullshit stories, and then sit in on a few games with them. Pros don't cheat. You can't cheat on TV, and they're all gutless college boys, anyway. Because they don't cheat, they are risking money every time they sit at the table. The best players in the world don't win every time. They're happy for the chance to lecture about how to win. It's a good payday without risk.

It can be a great payday for you, too—if you get into those seminars, you'll find a lot of players who think they're better than they are. They're willing to lay out a nice hunk of change to learn from the best. They'll get more confident after the seminar, and you want to make sure you get friendly with all of them. Then, clean them out.

In this day and age, I think some new ballsy hotshot kid will take the time to learn everything I'm teaching, then try to put these lessons to work as a pro. Maybe he'll get famous. The TV cameras will be burning his hands all the time, and sooner or later he'll get fucked for cheating on television. Or, maybe that'll make him a superstar. I don't know shit about TV. I never met anyone who liked *Friends*.

Let's not forget online poker. How many fucking poker Web sites are there? Not one of them is legal in the USA. They're all offshore, and until the government figures out they can make a mint by making them legal and taxing them, these Web sites will keep springing up. What a priceless idea that is. Playing poker online. You send them money and they tell you what your cards are, then they tell you whether you won or not. That's a nifty idea. Why the fuck didn't I think of that? (I did. See below.*) On top of it all, the sites take a hefty rake.

Online is not a good place for cheats because everyone is cheating. You sure as hell can't get readers in play or do any mechanic's work; all you can do is collusion. You can collude with yourself by setting up three or four accounts. You can start a table where you're playing three or four seats. You can drive anyone out. If whipsawing doesn't scare people away, you'll still win by knowing half the cards that are in play by playing half of the seats.

But I don't like it. It seems like cheating for amateurs. Everyone is cheating in online poker and they're not really cheaters. They're the wrong kind of people. They're people who don't even think they're cheating; they see it as an understood part of the game. I've heard all sorts of excuses. If you're going to cheat, whip out your prick and cheat like a man. If you can't face the man you're stealing money from eye-to-eye, you ain't a mover in my book. You also won't make anywhere near as much money on a computer. Online is for weasels and pussies.

....

* I came up with the idea for online poker even before computers were invented. I had a postal-mail game years ago. I mailed out cards to six guys, and they'd mail back their bets and envelopes full of cash. The winner of each hand got the cash. I wasn't playing; I was just dealing, so why would I cheat? I kept all the money. It was just a few bucks and mostly I did it as a joke; I got a kick out of seeing how gullible people could be. I thought you could never get any real card action from a distance, but Internet gambling is huge. If one of these online companies skips out with all the money after a few years, I'll be really impressed.

It's not all bad, though. Online games aren't killing real poker, they're making it more popular. People get the itch to play, and once they think they know shit about the game, they'll be looking to play for real. You get to cheat them for real, and you take their real money. Technology is a beautiful thing.

Chapter 32

THE TEMPTATION TO PLAY FAIR—
JULIA ROBERTS IS STILL A WHORE

Between playing poker every night, and usually knowing what people have in their hands, you're going to become a very good poker player. Everyone else you're playing against is playing once every couple of weeks. They aren't paying attention like they should and they don't know what other people are holding. You'll be better than everyone you play against. You're going to be a fine honest poker player on your way to becoming a great crooked poker player.

At some point, you will be tempted to stop cheating and play square. You'll think that you might feel better about yourself. You might think about going on television and becoming a big poker star. Don't fall for that shit. It'll fuck you up. It's not right.

I'm a great fucking poker player. I can beat any of the pros. If I went on TV now and played fair, I'd still have all the rich assholes wanting to play with me, and I could beat their asses and make them thank me for every bad beat like a pansy boy paying to be spanked. But I don't play square. You can't pay me enough.

Did you see that piece-of-shit movie *Pretty Woman*? That movie is phony bullshit. And it's not fake because there aren't hookers who are better-looking than Julia Roberts. I've had many with much better bodies who didn't have that fucking carp mouth on them. Who needs a mouth that size? Johnny Wadd is dead.

No, the bullshit of *Pretty Woman* isn't that a hooker can't be a piece of ass. It's not even that a rich guy wouldn't marry a hooker. A lot of rich assholes would be happy to marry a hooker. They have skills.

I played cards with a filthy rich record producer in Jersey. I took a truckload of money from him, but I still didn't touch the price he forked over to a drug dealer for one band's high for one session. It didn't take much cheating to make money off of him. He didn't care about winning; he just wanted to talk about himself.

This record producer, let's call him Ringo—because that would make him happy—was getting a lot of shit from one of the guys because Ringo was fucking a porn star. Ringo finally looked at him and said, "You've been to my studio, right? I got a tape recorder in my studio. How much use do you think that tape recorder gets? We all use it every day and we use it hard. Different bands come in, different engineers come in, and they all use that tape recorder. They use it all the time, every day, all day and all night. You got a tape recorder in your home, don't you? You use it once in a while, right? Of course you do. Which would you rather use? Mine or yours? Which recorder would you trust to be working right all the time? Exactly. When you make money with something, you take care of it. That's why I'm happy fucking porn stars and hookers—they take care of their shit."

Hookers can be better-looking than Julia Roberts. Rich guys can fall in love with hookers and marry them. Those aren't lies. The lie is that you can be happier going straight. Honest people use that lie to protect themselves. Squares think it's fun not to know everything that's going on. They think it's fun not to be in control. Hookers and cheaters know things are better if someone is running the show. You can be much happier as a whore or a cheat. You have to accept who you are. If you're a hooker, be a fucking hooker. If you're a junkie, be a junkie. You bought this book because you want to be a cheat, so be a cheat and stay a cheat.

When I'm cheating at a table, I am god. I know things that no one else knows. I see everything and I take care of everybody. If I see one guy starting to get pissed, I dump a pot to him and cheer him up. If another guy is being an asshole, I fuck him on the river. I watch everyone's mood. I don't kill the golden goose; I make sure everyone has fun. My games have structure. There's a great story in every game. There's a feeling to my tables. I'm in control. I take care of my suckers. I teach them lessons in how to treat people. I take their money and give them a great night of poker. They need me. They love me.

Whenever I've played fair, it was cold and random. I still won money, but sometimes it would be from the wrong guy. Sometimes an asshole would get lucky and make more than he should. Sometimes a guy who couldn't afford it would go down hard and never play again. Fair play isn't fair; it needs a guiding hand.

You can make money playing fair, but it isn't right. Someone has to be in control and that someone is me. That someone could be you. We'll deal from the basement, they'll love us, and Julia Roberts can suck my cock.

ACKNOWLEDGMENTS

I'm not a guy who's grateful to a lot of people. That's because everything I've got, I got on my own thanks to my own hard work and talent. I've always worked alone. I didn't have a book to help me. But that doesn't matter. Thank-yous are a good idea, because if I've taught you anything, it's that you should keep people happy, and if a few insincere words fill the bill, why the hell not?

I could start by thanking every single person I've cheated over the years, but I don't remember any of their names, so fuck them. They're all blurry images to me, just sacks of money with hair and clothes. I remember the ridiculous-looking ones, the ugly ones, but I don't waste brain space on their names. If I'd known I was going to write this book, I would have kept a list of them all. For all I care, they all have the same name: Mark. When I burn a game, I burn them out of my memory. While I'm playing, I know everything about them. Where did they go to school? What's their wife's name? What's their favorite brand of whiskey? Once I'm done, I forget all the boring details of their boring lives, and I'm glad I don't have to hear from them again. I kiss the cards that I don't have to live their lives.

I'd really like to thank whoever it was that's responsible for the explosion in the popularity of poker. For years and years, whenever the *World Series of Poker* was happening, I'd see a nice bump in profits. Once in a while, a movie about poker would show up and my job would get a little easier for a while. But, when poker started to get TV time, every idiot and his brother wanted to play at home. Poor people (fuck you), rich people (thank you), and everyone in between (fuck you, thank you). The last few years have been amazing. I guess the nice thing about the game is that when people see it on television, they think they can play it, too. It's not football or log rolling; you don't need skill or talent, right? You can sit at home and think you're just as good as those pros, and all you have to do is push some chips around. All you need is a little bit of money and you can make a lot. Great. You're right. Keep coming.

Penn Gilette *[it's Jillette, amazing]* and Mickey Lynn should get a lot of thanks. Penn owed me and he must have something on Lynn. They're pains in my ass, but they got everything together, and they saved me from dealing with any asshole publishers. I only dealt with those two. They asked a lot of questions and they worked harder on the book than I did. They wrote most of the fucker. But I'm the one who spent all those years learning all the shit and taking all the beatings. They made the book easy to read, but I lived the fucker.

Zoe in Pittsburgh gets a thank-you, because she told me that if she ever got her name in print, she'd live forever, and when I told her I could make it happen, she offered me free suckoffs for life. Open wide, Zoe.

Thanks to J.C., who went from being a tough motherfucking lawbreaker to a hardworking citizen (but still a tough motherfucker), and then went too early to the dirt. He meant the world to me and got me out of more than one tight spot. He was the nuts. His bottom deal was so good that I changed mine to his. He taught me something. I love you, Jerry.

There is one guy I played with, his initials are J. B. He's about the only guy I ever cheated that I remember fondly. I got in big trouble and even though he knew I was guilty, he stood up for me. J. B. let himself get beat up rather than let someone beat on me, even though I'd taken his money, too. That gave me time to get away with several grand. I would never have done that for him. What an idiot. But a true stand-up guy.

I also want to thank you for reading this book. It's going to make us both a lot of coin, in more ways than you'll ever know.

—Dickie Richard

I'm sure that if Dickie knew the hard work that Kim Scheinberg, Elizabeth Beier, Dan Strone, Krasher Lewis, Glenn Alai, Diane Lewis, and Emily Zolten Jillette put into this book, he would thank them as well.

And if you believe that, let's play some cards.

—Penn Jillette

GLOSSARY

People really do talk like this. No shit. I don't like to, but if you need some character for one of your games or if you don't understand some of the shit I'm slinging in the book, this might help you.

Aces and spaces—Two aces with three rags.

Ace him out—Beat someone on a hand with an ace-high.

Aces up—Two pairs, one of which is aces.

Acey-deucy—A–2 in hole; also, a quick game (sometimes called "Red Dog") where you bet that card number three will fall between cards number one and two (dealt faceup).

Action—The level of excitement (and, more important, betting) of a game.

Add-'Em-Up Lowball—Draw poker where the hand with the least number of points wins.

Advantage player—A cowardly cheat; usually someone who thinks that anything that anyone at the table can do is just "advantage play," not cheating, including glimpsing a card you're not supposed to see. If you're going to cheat, be a man and cheat.

Advantage tool—A hold-out machine, or a bug.

Advertising—Giving people the impression that you're a weak player to get more action later on. You might show hands like K–4, a gutshot straight draw, or a middle pair; people don't revise their first impressions very often.

A-game—The highest stakes game. *Opposite of* Z-game.

Ainsworth—2–6 as hole cards. Named after some asshole, I guess.

Air—Some guys put a lot of air into their hands. (They don't protect the cards properly; they expose them to too much air.)

Ajax—A–J as hole cards.

Alabama night riders—Three kings.

Alcohol—An annoying way to say "I'll call."

Alexander—King of clubs.

All-in—To bet every chip in one bet. You take your money, and you put all of it in the pot. This is very scary unless you know you're going to win. That's why you have this book—to take away that fear.

All red (all black, all green, all purple, all blue)—A flush.

AMC—Abbreviation of "all my chips."

American Filthy Monk—A version of Hold 'Em with the jack of spades wild when it's a hole card. Keeping that card on the bottom can be useful to get the betting up.

Ammo—Slang for chips. ("I need more ammo.")

Angle—A method to up your profits that's not technically against the rules but is clearly not in the spirit of the game.

Angle shooter—A person who barely plays in the limits of the rules; just shy of being a cheat; a cheater with no balls.

Ante bean—A chip used for the ante.

Apology card—Looking at the next card in the deck, if you missed your hand, to see what you might have gotten. Also called "rabbit hunting."

Apple—An unusually big money game.

Argine—The queen of clubs.

Arkansas flush—A four-card flush; it's sometimes given value in home games.

Around the corner straight—Home games sometimes allow hands to wrap around an ace-high, like Q–K–A–2–3.

Artist—A cheat who manipulates the deck through sleight of hand.

Axe—A rake or a drop; a percentage taken by the house each hand. Sometimes home games will try to have an axe. The guy who runs this kind of setup is going to make money by hosting the game; he becomes a casino and is ripping you off by cutting into your profits.

B-dealer—Bottom dealer. Just be one, don't talk about it. Also called "Subway dealer", "Cellar dealer."

Back door flush—Catching two cards to complete a flush (or straight).

Backlining—An agreement between two (or more) players to make a separate stack of chips; for each hand won, a certain number of chips are put in the backline. At some point later, the two players split the line. This is illegal in most card clubs. You want to always play tight and get a backline partner who is a loose player; they'll be playing in more pots, and therefore winning more pots, and you get chips whether those wins are big or small.

Back peek—Squeezing the deck with thumb and little finger to bow up top card and get a glimpse; done prior to dealing seconds.

Back raise—In games where there's a limit to the number of raises in a round, but not a rule that raises have to be at least as big as raises already made, a back raise is a small raise to hit the cap without spending much money.

Bad beat—An unlucky event. When you are a huge favorite to win a hand and your opponent gets the only card that can help him on the river, you are the victim of a bad beat. You will be giving bad beats to the people you play against on a regular basis.

Baggage—A person who hangs around a game but has no money to play.

Baker—Second position to the left of the dealer.

Bar (barred)—Banned.

Barnburner—Excellent hand (such as four aces or a straight flush).

Baseball—A stud game with 3s and 9s wild.

Basement dealing—Dealing from the bottom.

Bedsprings—A version of Cincinnati with ten community cards faceup.

Beer hand—2–7 unsuited (the worst hand in Hold 'Em: go get a beer).

Behind a log—When one player is way ahead in chips and decides to play only premium hands.

Belly-up—To play honestly; playing belly-up. Also means broke, for very good reason.

Best hand—A form of collusion without raising; partners signal and the one with the best hand stays in, the other one folds. Most common in hi-lo games.

Bet or get—A home game rule that has you bet or fold, no checking allowed.

Big bobtail—A four-card open-ended straight flush.

Big dime—$10,000.

Big dog—Five cards from ace through 9 with no pairs.

Big nickel—$500.

Big slick—A–K as hole cards. A lot of players will never lay down this hand in Hold 'Em because they think it's too valuable to throw away; you can use this to your advantage—this is a good hand to deal to your geese. Named after a big fucking oil slick in Alaska (AK).

Big Squeeze—Six-card hi-lo stud with one twist.

Bike (wheel)—A–2–3–4–5 straight.

Bitch—Queen.

Black chip game—One that uses only $100 chips.

Blackleg—Cheater.

Blaze—A nonstandard hand, valued between two pair and three of a kind, made up of all face cards (no pair).

Bleed—Win a lot of money a little bit at a time.

Blind bet—A player who is first to act may make a bet before he looks at his cards or at the next community card.

Blinds—Forced bets made before the deal of each hand to stimulate betting. The "small blind" is a half bet and is made by the player on the dealer's left. The "big blind" is a full bet and is made by the player two positions to the left of the dealer.

Blistering—The marks put on cards. *See* Pegging.

Blivit—A totally worthless hand.

Block—A worthless watch (similar to a hoop). People try to sell these in card rooms, or they can be offered as collateral on a loan that will never be paid back.

Blockout work—Marking the cards by filling in part of the pattern on the back.

Blocky—6–3 as first two cards.

Blow back—To lose profits, usually from sticking around too long.

Bolt—To fold.

Bone—A $1 chip (white).

Boost—To raise.

Bottom pair—Lowest pair on the board.

Bouble Bluff—Bluff made by betting, getting raised, then reraising.

Bounty—Money paid for eliminating another player. This is usually done in tournaments, but a lot of people will offer bounties in freeze-outs.

Boxed card—An upside-down card in the deck.

BR—Bankroll.

Brass Brazilians—The nuts.

Break—Win all of someone's chips. ("I broke Boomer and sent him home crying to his wife.")

Breastworks—A hold-out machine worn under a vest or jacket.

Breathe—To pass on the first chance to bet.

Brief—A tiny stepping of the cards in the deck for a cut, so your partner can return cards to the order you want them in.

Bring in—Open (a pot).

Brush off—A sign given in poker rooms when management spots a cheat and wants them to leave, but they don't want to alert their customers that a cheater's been playing in their establishment. They'll make a brushing motion of one hand down the other arm below the elbow or across the other hand, or sometimes across the upper lip. If they do this to you, leave right away. It might be a good time to go home and practice.

Buck—A dollar, or sometimes $100. People call dollars "bucks" because they used a buck knife as a dealer button in the old days (before my time). The knife got replaced by a silver dollar, but they still called it a buck. Who said that cheaters don't know shit?

Bug—(1) A cheating device that holds a card on the underside of a table. (2) A term for the joker. Some people think "bug" and "joker" mean the same thing, but others think of a bug as a wild card that can only be used to complete a straight or a flush (a semi-wild card). You can turn this confusion over what a bug is to your advantage.

Bullet—An ace.

Bully Johnson—3–5 as the first two cards.

Bump—To raise.

Burn—(1) To muck the top card before dealing the flop, turn, or river. This prevents players from seeing marks on the top card of the deck. (2) To stare at a player's hands intensely, looking for sleight of hand. (3) To abandon a poker game and never come back, if you think you may get caught or there's no more money to be made. (4) A full house.

Burn card—A card that's dealt facedown into the muck; it's standard practice in games like Hold 'Em to burn the top card of the deck before each street. It's supposed to stop cheaters. It doesn't work.

Bust (bust out)—To lose.

California—A home game where each player gets five cards, plus five cards in the widow in the center of the table. There's a round of betting before the first widow is turned up, and a bet after each subsequent round (eleven bets). The best five-card hand made from the hole cards and the widow wins. Also called "Lamebrains," or "Utah."

Calamity Jane—Queen of spades.

Call someone down—Check or call every bet all the way to the river.

Calling station—A very loose player who will call any bet.

Canine—K–9 hole cards.

Card mob—A team of card cheats.

Carding—Noticing exposed cards for advantage play.

Carpet—The price of 3 to 1.

Carry a slug—To insert a slug of cards (for example, several spades) into the deck for dealing out later.

Case bet—A gambler's last bet of the night, when he's lost his entire stake.

Cat flush (tiger flush)—A nonstandard hand that consists of five cards, all of one suit, 3 to 9, with no straight or pair. This is ranked above a straight flush in home games. *See* Tiger.

Century—$100 bill.

Chaffer—A hack cheat; someone who thinks he's a master card mechanic, but he's just another sucker.

Chalk eater—Someone who only bets on favorites. "All the chalk eaters are putting money on me to win."

Charles (Charlemagne)—King of hearts.

Charlie—The third position to the left of the dealer, also called "under the gun."

Chase (chase a bet)—To continue to bet in a pot on a very weak draw in the hopes that everyone folds to you or that you hit your hand. You want to find people who chase their bets, because those people are used to losing a lot of money.

Cheaters—Marked cards.

Check cop—(1) One who steals chips out of the pot. (2) The sticky substance (glue) used to make chips stick to your hand so you don't have to palm them (for amateurs only).

Chicago—Seven Card Stud where a high spade in the hole wins half the pot.

Chicago bankroll—Same as a Michigan bankroll: a roll of singles with a fifty- or a hundred-dollar bill on the outside. It's good for a diversion; always have one with you. Chuck it away from you, run the other way.

Chicken picken—A poker variation with eleven cards: Deal two cards per player; three rows of three make up the widow.

Chingaderos—The nuts.

Chip race—In freeze-outs or home tournaments, the host might decide to do a chip race to get rid of the smaller chips on the table. You "chip up" to the next values. All the odd chips are either put in the next pot or high card gets them.

Chip-rack—To be asked to leave, to put all your chips in the rack and get out. ("I was chip-racked once because I got busted by a hanger.")

Chippy—A poker player who stinks at the game.

Chop—(1) To return the blinds to the players who posted them if no one calls the hand. Don't do it. (2) An offer to split a pot before a showdown. This is a good thing to suggest a lot; people will usually be nice and take you up on it, and you won't be seen as winning as many pots. Even though you'll make half as much money, it pays off in table perception.

Chops—Skills. You'll need perfect chops with a deck of cards before you sit across from anyone.

Chump—Anyone who sits down at the table with you.

Chute—On fancy tables, the slot in the drop box where the money gets pushed in.

Cinch—The best hand. A sure winner.

Cincinnati—A ten-card poker game with five cards per hand and five in the widow.

Cincinnati Liz—A version of Cincinnati where the widow card with the lowest value is wild.

Class—The rank of a hand.

Clean—Straight. Honest. Stupid.

Clean move—A perfectly done sleight-of-hand move.

Clean up (clean out)—Take a lot (or all) of your opponents' money.

Clip—To cheat someone out of their money.

Closed card—A down card.

Closed poker—Any flavor of poker that has all the cards facedown. Closed poker games (like Five Card Draw) aren't ideal because the other players will have a tougher time guessing at the strength of your hand. There are no faceup community cards.

Coat card—Old term for face cards (they wear coats).

Cockle—Price of 10 to 1.

Coffeehousing—Acting in a way that's the opposite of how you feel. When someone tries to sound sincere while congratulating you after you bust their big hand, they're coffeehousing. When you act angry after "losing" an "unlucky" hand, you're coffeehousing.

Cold—(1) Unlucky. (2) A slow game. (3) Getting three cards in a row (three cold aces).

Cold deck—A prestacked deck. A cold deck is literally colder than the cards in play, which have warmed up a bit as they've been used. Before you switch your cold deck for the deck in play, you want to keep your cold deck close to you so it stays warm, but not too warm. A jacket pocket is good.

Come back on (come back at)—Reraise. You want to come back at people when they're set up with the second-best hand.

Come off—To split up a hand in order to draw for a higher-value hand; for example, in Five Card Draw, if you're dealt 6–6–5–4–3, you would come off by drawing for the straight instead of keeping the 6–6.

Common card—A community card, usable by all players.

Community cards—Flop, widow, etc. Cards that can be used by anyone at the table to make their hand.

Complimentary play—Dumping hands to make someone feel better after a big loss; a bit of a payback to keep them coming back for more.

Confederate (agent)—Secret partner. You don't want to work with confederates; they cut into your profits.

Contract—A declaration of high or low at the end of a split pot.

Copping from the pot—To steal chips from the pot, right under their noses, without getting caught. If you get caught, it's not "copping from the pot," it's a fucking death wish.

Cosmetics—Paint; daub; markings on the back.

Counter—A chip.

Counting down the stub—Counting the remaining cards in the deck after the deal to see if someone's holding out. You should get good at this.

Cow—To "go cow" is to have someone split the buy-in for a game with you, then split the winnings at cash-out.

Cowboy—(1) A king. (2) A very loose player.

Crabs—3–3 as hole cards. 3 is referred to as "a crab" by people wanting to sound hip.

Crack—To beat a powerful hand.

Crazy Otto—Five Card Stud with lowest card wild.

Crazy Pineapple—A variation of pineapple. *See* Pineapple.

Crier—A loser who complains about losing. Most criers are easy to put on tilt; hand them a small loss, then a small win, and then give them decent cards and they'll usually bet big.

Cripple—Destroy the chance of getting action on a hand because you have the cards that would make someone else a hand. For example, you have A–A and the flop has A–A; everyone is afraid of an ace and won't play. Also called "Cripple the deck."

Crisscross—A poker game; same as Cincinnati, but the five cards in the widow are laid out in an X with the center card wild. *Similar to* Southern Cross.

Cross lift—A two-man cheating system where the cheat with the best hand signals to his partner to raise back and forth, squeezing out callers. *Similar to* Whipsaw.

Crossroader—A cheater.

Cross-staking—You get two people (or more) to bankroll you in the same game without them knowing about each other. You agree to give each of them a percentage of your winnings. If each gives you $500 for the same night's buy-in, you pocket $500 and lose that night.

Cull—To get cards out of the deck (without being noticed).

Curse of Mexico—Two of spades.

Curse of Scotland—Nine of diamonds.

Cutoff seat—The person to the right of the dealer. When you control who you sit next to, don't put a chatty person on your right; when you're dealing, a chatty person draws attention and you want them far away from you while you're working.

Dame—Queen. *See* Bitch.

Dark—Not looking at the cards. ("I'll play this hand dark.")

David—King of spades.

Dead man's hand—Black aces, black eights, nine of diamonds . . . Wild Bill Hickok was holding these cards when he was shot dead.

Deadwood—Used cards that are out of play (or culled cards that you drop on the floor).

Dealer button—A white disc that shows who is dealing. In casinos, one dealer handles the job for each person playing—the button moves clockwise around the table. In home games, people usually pass the deck around, but nowadays it's popular to use a button even if you don't need one, because people see them on TV.

Dealer's Choice—In this game, in each hand, the dealer chooses which game to play.

Dean (professor)—A gambler who can calculate the odds. These guys are great to play with, because they understand that a 95 percent favorite still loses 5 percent of the time, and they keep playing when it happens.

Deep—Amount of betting committed in a hand. "How deep are you?" means how much do you have invested so far.

Dent (round)—Making an impression in a card with a fingernail.

Deuce dealer (number two man)—A dealer who deals seconds.

Deuces wild—Any 2s are treated as wild cards.

Devil's bedposts—4 of clubs.

Dewey—In draw poker, a way to tell the dealer "Give me two cards."

Dig—To get more money from someone's pocket during a game; in cardrooms and casinos you can only play what's on the table, but in home games you can often dig.

Dime—$1,000.

Doctored cards—Marked cards.

Doctor Pepper—Seven Card Stud with 2s, 4s, and 10s wild.

Doghouse cut—Any cut that splits the deck into more than two stacks; this is an unusual move, but makes for very simple false cutting.

Dollar—$100, or a $100 bill. A dime is more than a dollar in card slang. So is a big nickel.

Dolly Parton—9–5 as starting hand. Some guys love this cutesy shit. From the movie *9 to 5* that she starred in.

Dominated hand—A hand that will very rarely win against another hand; A–K dominates K–2. It's good to play dominated hands like K–J versus K–Q, because people won't give them up.

Doped cards—Cards marked on the back with ink, bleach, or water.

Double-Barreled Shotgun—A poker game that's a cross between Draw and Stud. *Also called* Texas Tech.

Double Belly-Buster—A straight draw with two holes: 5–7–8–9–J. 6 or 10 makes a straight. Good to set up this hand, give your sucker a 6, and keep the 10 for yourself, or 10–Q.

Double Draw London Lowball—A variation on London Lowball.

Double off—Two good hands are dealt, the better one going to the dealer or his accomplice.

Double-pop—Reraise. He bet, Slim raised, I double-popped him.

Down the river—Seven Card Stud.

Down to the felt—A player who has lost most of his chips is down to the felt.

Doyle Brunson—10–2 hole cards. Doyle Brunson won two *World Series of Poker* with this hand, catching a full house each time. You'll never want to appear to be that fucking lucky.

Drag—Pull in the chips after winning a pot.

Drawing dead—Trying to win a hand that can't be won.

Drib—A bad player.

Drink pot—An agreement that the next pot (or a portion of it) will be spent to buy everyone drinks. Always win this hand. People bet looser (more money) and you'll get a lot of bonus points for buying people a round.

Drum—A very tight player, tight as a drum.

Duke—(1) To muck your cards. (2) Shortchange a pot by holding chips back.

Dumb end—The weak end of a straight. You have 2–3 and the flop is 4–5–6; a 7–8 beats you.

Dummy up—Shut up, quit talking. You should dummy up about cheating if you're going to cheat and not get caught.

Dump—To lose a hand on purpose. It may feel wrong to ever lose a pot, but it's an important part of being a good cheater. If they never win, they won't keep playing. Winning one out of a hundred hands is enough to keep most players coming back week after week. *Also called* Complimentary play.

Dutch straight—An every-other-card straight sometimes played in home games: 2–4–6–8–10, 3–5–7–9–J. Ace is usually high, but sometimes both high and low. A Dutch straight ranks higher than three of a kind, but lower than a straight. *Also called* a Skip straight, or Kilter.

Dynamite—A variety of poker played with only two cards.

Edge work—A way of marking cards on the sides by sanding them down.

Elevator the cut—Perform a pass to undo a cut.

Elimination—A version of poker similar to Cincinnati, but cards in any hand that match widow cards are eliminated from play. *Also called* Weary Willie.

Elk river—A hand with three 10s.

Elmer—Sucker, chump.

Eubie—8–6 as starting cards. Comes from saying "If you play 8–6, you be broke."

Exposure—How much money you could possibly lose in a game; in Hold 'Em, your exposure is how much money you've got plus the amount of credit they'll give you.

Eyes—A–A in the hole; also called "American Airlines," "pocket rockets," "bullets," "Eyes of Texas."

Fairbanking—Dumping hands to an opponent so he thinks he's on a lucky streak or believes he's a good player.

The farm—All one's chips. Also called "the ranch."

Fat—Having money.

Feeble Phoebe—A poker game similar to Hollywood, but its hi-lo and community cards are turned over two at a time.

Feeding the kitty—Calling a lot of bets.

Feeler bet—An exploratory bet; trying to see if people will raise or fold with a small amount of action.

Feelout game—A game that lets you test the waters and see if the fish are biting. It's just research. You can invest a few bucks to find out if there's real money to be made.

Fever—A card or bet with a value of five.

Fifth street—The fifth community card in Hold 'Em. *Also called* the river.

Fin—Five dollars.

Finky dink—8–5 in the hole.

Fire—To raise, or to make an aggressive bet.

Fishhooks—J–J in the hole.

Five-minute rule—A rule called against players who spend too long trying to decide what to do. If it's imposed and the time is up, the player folds. This is good to put pressure on slow players, which forces them to rush, puts them on tilt, and helps you get in more hands.

Fix the deck—Stack the deck in a prearranged order.

Flat—Crooked, dishonest. Any game you're in will be a flat game.

Flat limit—A game in which every bet and raise is the same preset amount.

Flicker Flicker—Five card hi-lo stud.

Flop—First three community cards. Used as a verb, too: "He flopped a king."

Flush—(1) Five cards of the same suit. (2) Having a lot of cash: "It's payday and he's flush."

Follow the rabbit—A way of getting more action by having everyone kick in some money to a pot that's won when someone wins two other pots in a row.

Forest—Three 3s (a lot of trees).

Fourth street—The fourth community card in Hold 'Em. *Also called* the turn.

Freak hand—A nonstandard poker hand like a blaze, skip straight, big dog, little tiger, etc.

Free look—Seeing a community card without anyone betting.

Freeze-out—Last man standing gets all the money. It's not a bad strategy to go out first in a freeze-out game. Grab the money box and leave while everyone else is playing.

Fucker—Someone who you dump an opening hand to (in order to increase the action) and who then takes the money, cashes out, and leaves.

Fuzz—Fake overhand shuffle that doesn't change the card order.

G-note—A $1,000 bill.

Gaff—Gimmicked or rigged cards, or any other cheating device.

Gambler's Last Charge—A poker game with five cards per hand and five widow cards; the last community card turned up is wild if it matches a card in a player's hand.

Gaper—*See* shiner. Also called a "reflector," or "gleamer."

Gay waiter—A three with a queen. A three is a trey, and a queen is a queer. So, a queen with a trey (tray) is a gay waiter. Really cute, if you're a fucking asshole.

Geese—Suckers.

George—Good or great. ("This is a George game.") *Opposite of* Tom.

German virgins—9–9 as a starting hand. (Nein! Nein!)

Gleek—Three of a kind.

Go south—(1) Remove chips or cards from the table.
(2) Disappear completely (yourself); burn town.

Golden chairs—Poker played with four hole cards and three community cards, with the lowest hole card sometimes played as wild.

Golyoonies—The nuts, the best hand.

Goolsby—Q–10 as a starting hand.

Gorillas—K–K as starting hand (King Kong).

Grand jury—Three 4s. (A grand jury has twelve members.)

Granny Herschel—A version of Cincinnati for four, six, or eight players: half the players make single bets in a round, and the other half make double bets; the winner takes the full pot. *Also called* Two Limit Granny Herschel.

Gravy—Extra, unexpected profit.

Grease—A bribe. Grease palms for information from locals (barbers, bartenders, etc.) about good games in town.

Greek—A thief or card sharp.

Grifter—Poker cheat.

Grind—Win small amounts consistently but over a long, slow period.

Gut shot—A draw that fills an inside straight. (Getting a 5 when you hold 3–4–6–7 is a gut-shot straight draw.)

Half a dollar—A fifty-dollar bill. Also called "half a yard."

Half smart—Partially aware of cheater's techniques, but not completely in the know.

Hammer—Last person to bet in a round. ("You've got the hammer.")

Handful—Price of 5 to 1.

Hanger—A card that accidently slides out of the bottom of the deck when dealing from the basement, tipping the move. You should never have a hanger; if you do, go back and practice, and then practice some more.

Hard (and soft)—If you ask for twenty hard and eighty soft, that means twenty in cash and eighty chips from a $100 bill.

Have a sign on your back—To be known as a cheat. You never want to have a sign on your back.

Heads-up—Play between only two players.

Heavy—A bad card. "I caught heavy" means I missed my hand by a lot.

Heavy deck—A deck that's got more than fifty-two cards in it. Most people won't notice this—unless, for example, two kings of diamonds show up in one hand.

Hector—Jack of diamonds.

Heef a dooler—Fifty cents. Don't waste time with bullshit heef-a-dooler pots.

Heeler—A kicker.

Hen—Queen.

Here to there—A straight.

Hidden declarations—In hi-lo, a way to declare by holding a chip of a certain color in your hand.

High breeze hummer—A very tight player. They're easier to clean, because when they finally do get the good cards, they make bigger bets.

High Chicago—A great Seven Card Stud variant where the highest spade in the hole gets half the pot. If you have the ace, you know you've won at least half. You'll get the ace.

High Mambo—A three-card poker game with one widow card; each player makes the best three-card hand from their three hole cards and one community card. Highest hand is A-K-Q suited. Next best hands (from high to low) are straight flush, three of a kind, straight, flush, one pair, high card.

High-roll—To bump up the stakes, or to bet more than anyone else is comfortable calling; either allows you to steal blinds. High-rolling is a good way to set up people who are afraid of high stakes; they'll call you when they think they have the cards. (If you high-roll for several hands in a row, this is how people will try to stop you.)

High roller—A high-stakes gambler.

Hilo Pocalo—A version of stud where the up cards can be passed to the player on your left.

Hit and run—To win a big pot after a short time and then hastily run on out the door.

Hitchhiker—Someone who unexpectedly stays in a pot when other players have big hands. It pays off to be a lucky hitchhiker who makes his hand on the river.

Hit the brief—Forcing a cut to a desired location.

Hockey sticks—7–7 in the hole.

Hogier—Jack of spades.

Hold 'Em—Seven-card game with two hole cards and five widow cards. Right now, the hottest game thanks to endless TV coverage. Originally called "Hold Me Darling," but no one wanted to ask to play that at a card table.

Hold-out—A card taken out of play and hidden for later use.

Hole cards—Facedown cards that each player is dealt. No one knows the value of anyone else's hole cards. Except, of course, you. *Also called* Pocket Cards.

Hollywood—(1) A show-off move. Great for setting yourself up as an ignorant chump. (2) Overbetting (or overacting). (3) A version of Cincinnati with fifteen cards, five in each hand and ten widow cards.

Holy city—The nuts.

Holy Nun Limit Heartaches—A version of Limit Hold 'Em where the queen of hearts, or any three hearts on the board, changes the game to no limit for that hand.

Honest readers—A fair deck of cards that has imperfections in it. You can use it just as well as marked cards.

Honor card—Any card 10 or higher.

Hook—A jack.

Hooker—Queen.

Hoop—A worthless ring, often sold in card rooms; good for collateral in home games on a loan you'll never pay back.

HORSE—A game where several poker variations are played in rotation, one each deal: Limit Hold 'Em, Omaha, Razz, Seven Card Stud (high), and Seven Card Stud Hi-Lo (Eight-or-better).

Horsing—Passing a small amount of money to another player after you win a pot. People sometimes do this as a tip or a joke, or to pay back a loan.

Huey, Dewey, and Louie—Three deuces. Also called "ducks".

Humps—A form of strippers where the cards are shaved to make the middle of the long edge stick out so you can tell by feel what the card is. *See* Strippers.

Ice—A cold deck.

Immortal—Unbeatable hand, the nuts.

Imperfect deck—Due to flaws in the printing of cards, you may find markings on the deck that you didn't put on. They'll work just as well as marks you add yourself.

In front—Ahead in the money.

Index—The upper-left (and lower-right) corner of a playing card that shows you the rank and suit.

International signals—A set of signals that card cheats in this country and overseas all use. I'm not going to give you the list of signals; that's because you don't want to help these guys. Why share the winnings? And, more often than not, they aren't very good. You'll get busted in a card room or a casino for using those signals, and a savvy home player will take you outside and sit you down hard.

Iron duke—The nuts.

Irwin!—This is an insider's joke; when you reveal pocket 5s, you're supposed to say "Presto!" and the response is "Irwin!" It shows you're a poker geek.

Italian game—A game with only red, white, and green chips; those are the colors of the Italian flag.

Itemer—Someone who helps a cheat by sending signals or providing a cold deck.

Jack Benny—3–9 as hole cards; from a running joke Benny made about his age.

Jack it up—To raise.

Jam—To bet or raise the maximum (jam the pot).

Jerusalem—The nuts. *Also called* Holy city.

Jesse James—4–5 as hole cards; legend says he was shot with a .45; also, someone who steals pots.

Jitney—A $5 chip.

Jog—To put a step or break in the deck. You can use this to undo a cut later with a pass.

Johnny Moss—A–10 hole cards.

Judge Bean—Three 10s; named for some Old West judge who used to hand out a lot of thirty-day-or-thirty-dollar sentences.

Judith—Queen of hearts.

Juice—(1) The house percentage; *also called* Rake, Vig, or Vigorish. (2) A liquid used to mark cards. (3) Interest on money owed.

Kankakee—A variation of stud where everyone has access to a communal joker.

Kansas City Lowball—Deuce-to-Seven lowball. Joker is the lowest card not present in a hand. Best low hand is 2–3–4–5–7. Lowest hand wins.

Katie—K–10 hole cards.

Keep honest—To call an opponent on the river when you're probably beat, so you can see his cards and make sure he isn't bluffing. This is a good term to use if you enjoy irony.

Kelter—A nonstandard hand given value in home games. One (*also called* Pelter or Skeet) is a 9–5–2 with a card between 9 and 5 and another between 5 and 2 (e.g., 9–6–5–4–2). Another variation is no card higher than 9, no four flush, no pair, and no four straight. Kelter hands like skip or Dutch straights (2–4–6–8–10 or 5–7–9–J–K) are also called kilter hands. Ranks between three of a kind and a straight.

Kem—A brand of pro playing cards. These are plastic and a bit harder to mark than paper cards like Bicycles or Bees. People use them, so make sure you've practiced everything with them.

Kibitzer—A nonplaying observer; a railbird.

Kicker—The highest card that isn't part of making the hand; A–A–A–J–4 is a set of aces with a jack kicker.

Kick the Hoover—Someone who limps into a pot with a weak hand, hoping to suck out on the river and win.

Kilter—A Dutch straight or skip straight.

King crab—K–3 as hole cards.

King without a moustache—King of hearts.

Kitty—Sometimes refers to the pot, but also can refer to a collection made by all players for certain costs (food, beverages, cigarettes, etc). Don't forget to take the kitty, too.

Knave—Jack.

Knit—To sit around and wait; bide time until a good hand comes up.

Knuckle—Check.

Kokomo—K–8 as hole cards.

KYFMS—Tattoo this backward on your ass so you can read it in the mirror. It stands for "Keep Your Fucking Mouth Shut." Don't brag about cheating, don't confide in anyone, just stay quiet.

La Hire—Jack of hearts.

Lady—Queen.

Lamb—Sucker or mark, usually a poor player to boot.

Lamebrain Pete—A variation of Cincinati where the lowest widow card and all cards that match it are wild.

Lancelot—Jack of clubs.

Large—$1,000. "Three large" means three thousand dollars.

Lay down—To fold, or to show your cards during the showdown.

Lazy Pineapple—Poker variant where you make up the best hand from two out of three hole cards and five community cards.

Leather ass—Being patient (for good cards).

Lemon juice—Picking up the blinds without doing anything because everyone folds; a walk.

Lights—If a player is in a game that's not table stakes, he might not have enough in front of him to cover a bet. He takes out the number of chips from the pot that he's short and stacks them in front of him. If he wins, nothing happens. If he loses, he's got to pay back the lights to whoever won the pot.

Limpers—People who just call on bets; also called "limping in."

Liners—Face cards; you can see a line when you glimpse the corner.

Little black books—Any one of multiple different lowball games having one spade that's wild; Razz is the easiest real lowball variation to play with a wild card.

Little bobtail—A nonstandard hand that consists of a three-card straight flush; it usually ranks between two pair and three of a kind.

Little dog—Five cards 2 to 7 with no pair; ranks above straight, below big dog.

Little Minnie—Another name for a wheel; A–2–3–4–5.

Little tiger—Nonstandard hand with five cards between 3 and 9 with no pair; ranks above big dog and below big tiger.

Little Virginia—Poker variation; six card stud with low hole card wild.

Lobster—A sucker or mark.

Lock—A surefire hand, one that can't lose.

Locksmith—One who only plays the nuts (used as a put-down of another player).

Looking out the window—Not paying attention. You'll find a lot of guys looking out the window during long games, which is good for you.

Looloo—A freak hand allowed to win only once each night. Any random hand can be declared a looloo before play begins, such as four clubs and a spade.

Loose—A player who throws chips around too liberally trying to hit inside straights, flushes, and trying to match up any pair. They'll get lucky once in a while (in straight games) because they play more hands than other players. They'll also lose big.

Loose juice—Booze.

Lowball—A game where lowest hand wins; straights don't count. A–2–3–4–5 is the best low hand.

Lumberman's hand—2–4 (two-by-four).

Ma Ferguson—Five card stud with the lowest facedown card, and all like it, wild.

Mail—If you're caught bluffing, you can respond "You've been reading my mail" if you want to sound like a fool (and sometimes that's useful).

Major hand—Any hand containing a straight or better.

Make wages—To earn enough in a game so it's worthwhile.

Man with the axe—King of diamonds.

Marked cards—Cards that have been marked so you can tell the value and suit of each card by looking at the back of it. *Also called* Readers, Papers.

Marker—An IOU or a credit note. You can make a lot of money on markers with home games, especially if you never pay them off. If you're into extortion, threatening to show a marker to an employer or a wife if you're not paid a ridiculous amount of interest (that you never mentioned when you loaned the money) can be even more profitable.

Marriage—K–Q suited, as hole cards.

Mechanic—A guy who uses sleights to manipulate the cards; a second or bottom dealer, false shuffler, cut hopper, etc.

Meedle—A game where the stakes are raised but only for those players that want to raise the stakes; these hands can happen when all the lower-stakes players fold.

Mexican standoff—A split pot.

Mexican Stud—Five Card Stud where the cards are all dealt down and the player can choose his hole card. *Also called* Peep and Turn.

Michigan bankroll—A carny roll; single bills with one larger bill on the outside so it looks like a lot more money than it is. *Also called* Okie Bankroll.

Mighty Wurlitzer—8–8 as starting cards (there are eighty-eight keys on a piano).

Miles—A way of describing three of a kind. Three fours is twelve miles; three tens is thirty miles.

Milk the cards—To put cards in a desired location or order while shuffling them.

Minnow—Someone who is playing in a game way over his head; not enough money to compete.

Mitt joint—A crooked card room.

Molly Hogan—The queen of spades.

Monarch—A king.

Mongrel—K–9 as hole cards.

Monkey—Sucker; mark.

Montana Banana—9–2 as hole cards. Bananas will grow in Montana before you'll win with that hand. (Maybe not you, but other people.)

Mop squeezer—Queen.

Motherfucker—The word usually spoken by your opponent when you crack his nut flush with a full house. Jesus wouldn't be happy with that kind of language.

Motion—If you reach for your chips and someone says "The motion's good," that means they fold; any bet would have scared them out of the pot.

Motown—J–5 as hole cards (Jackson 5).

Mover—A card cheat.

Muck—To throw away cards into the discard pile.

Murder—A two- or six-card hi-lo game with up to four twists.

My Lord went thins—My luck ran out.

Nail—(1) A nail mark. (2) To catch someone cheating.

Natural—A hand that doesn't use any wild cards.

Needle—Someone who provokes another player through anger or sarcasm and puts him on tilt. One who does this is sometimes called a "needle artist."

Needles—Pair of aces.

Neves—Price of 7 to 1.

New Guinea Stud—A variation of Seven Card Stud that starts with four facedown cards, then two faceup cards, followed by a facedown card.

New York Stud—Five Card Stud where an Arkansas flush beats one pair.

Nickel—A $5 chip. Also called a "redbird."

Nigger Mike—Six-card draw with a bet on each card as it's dealt.

Nine-way hand—A four-card flush (there are nine other cards in the deck to complete the flush).

No Gypsy—A game in which you're not allowed to just call the big blind; if you're going to play, you've got to put in at least twice that amount.

No Peeky—A version of stud (five or seven) in which all cards are facedown. First player turns up one card and bets; next player turns over as many cards as he needs to beat the first player's exposed card, and bets. Play continues around the table. If five cards are turned over, that player is out.

No Room—You can say this when you have a full house, if you want to work the angle of being a fool.

Northern flight—Seven Card Stud with all hearts as wild cards, unless any spade is in the hand.

Nose—To play your own money (not house chips).

Nose wide open—Playing on tilt; also unglued, steaming.

Notch—To just barely beat someone. K–8, with a king high and an eight kicker, has just notched K–7.

Nubbin—A very small amount of money or chips.

Nuts—The best hand possible.

Office—A signal given by a card scammer to his partner. *See* Sign.

Office hours—Any hand made up of 9s and 5s, or a 5-to-9 straight.

Off-suit—Hole cards that aren't the same suit as each other.

Okie bankroll—Carny roll. Big bill folded on top of small bills to give the appearance of more money. *See also* Michigan Bankroll.

Oldsmobile—9–8 hole cards. (Little Oldsmobile is 8–8 hole cards.)

Omaha—Seven Card Stud with two hole cards and five community cards, rolled up one at a time. Only one hole card can be used to make the hand. Also called "Tight Hold 'Em."

On the rail—Out of the game, usually broke. Watching from the rail.

On the sleeve (on the cuff; on the finger)—Borrowing money to play. If you win, you pay back at the end of the session; if you lose, you'll settle up later. If you play on the sleeve, you'll "forget" to pay back at the end of the session, even if you do win.

One-eyed jacks—Jack of hearts and jack of spades. Usually heard when these are made wild cards.

One-shot—A game you will play in once and never come back. These games shouldn't take too much time to set up. Get as much money as you can and get out.

One-tooth—The second-best hand in Lowball.

One-way deck—Cards that have a pattern on the back that isn't the same when turned around. Cards with photos, for example, can all be lined up in the same direction, but you can turn around all the aces, making them easy to spot.

Option—If you're the big blind and no one has raised, when the betting comes back to you, you have the option of raising or checking.

Optional card—In stud, some games will allow the purchase of a "replacement card." You pay for it in the pot and get to replace any faceup card (with an up card) or facedown card (with a down card). *Also called* Twist.

Out—A card that can save your hand. If you have a gut-shot straight draw with 3–4–5–7, any 6 will be an out.

Pa Ferguson—Five Card Stud with high card and all its mates as wild.

Paint—Face cards.

Pallas—Queen of spades.

Palm—To hide chips or cards in the palm of your hand.

Palooka—A poor poker player.

Paper hanger—A person who writes bad checks on purpose.

Papers—Marked cards. *Also called* Readers.

Paper worker—A cheat who uses marked cards.

Pasadena—"I pass" as spoken by a moron who thinks he's an "insider."

Pasteboards—Cards.

Pat—To stay with the cards you have, standing pat.

Pedigree—K–9 as hole cards.

Peep and Turn—Five Card Stud where the cards are all dealt down and the player can choose his hole card. *Also called* Mexican Stud.

Pelter—Nonstandard hand given value in some home games, like a 9–5–2 with another card between 9 and 5 and another card between 5 and 2 with no pair.

Pickle Man—5–7 as hole cards (after the Heinz slogan "57 Varieties").

Pick up checks—A home game rule where you can increase your bet (in a limit game) once for every person who checks in front of you. If the limit is ten dollars and two people check before you get a chance to act, you can pick up their checks and come in for thirty dollars.

Picture cards—Face cards.

Pigeon—An inexperienced gambler; a sucker.

Pig in the poke—A wild widow card; every card like it is also wild.

Pig's eye—Ace of diamonds.

Pineapple—A variation of Hold 'Em where you get three hole cards, and either after the preflop betting or after the flop, you must discard one of your hole cards.

Pipe salesman—The term for a good and wise player who will tip other players off to cheats.

Pips—The spots on a card that show the value.

Pitch—"The twist"; an extra card that can sometimes be bought in home games of stud.

Play behind a log—When you're far ahead in chips, you can sit back and play only the best hands.

Ploppy—A player who doesn't know what he's doing.

Pocket cards—Hole cards.

Poke—Bankroll.

Pone—The player to the right of the dealer.

Post Oak Bluff—In no-limit, making a small bet in later rounds in the hopes that, out of fear that you're suckering them in, no one will raise you. Also called a "protection bet."

Pothook—Any 9.

Pot out—To take money out of the pot for food, drinks, or cigarettes.

Presto—Some people say this when they show pocket 5s in Hold 'Em; the "correct" response is to say "Irwin."

Producer—A player that has an unlimited bankroll and is happy to keep putting money into a game. Also called "provider."

Protecting your cards—To place a chip or a small object on top of your cards so that the dealer doesn't pull them into the muck. Most home games don't require you to protect your cards; most casinos do.

Pulling up—When one of your opponents leaves a game before you've taken all of his money, he's pulling up. This isn't always a bad thing: He might come back for more with a bigger bankroll.

Puppy feet—The suit of clubs, as referred to by someone who wants to sound like a retarded child.

Puta—Queen (Spanish for "whore").

Quads—Four of a kind.

Quint—Straight flush. You shouldn't see many of these, and you for damn sure shouldn't use a special word for them in a game.

Rabbit—A weak player. Also, a kitty that's awarded in home games to someone who wins two pots in a row.

Rabbit hunting—Turning over additional cards after a hand is over to see what would have happened if a player had called instead of folded. This is an excellent chance for side bets. Don't let someone take the card for free; offer them good odds that they won't see the card they want in the next five cards turned over. You make sure that they won't.

Rags—Worthless or low-value cards.

Railbirds—People who watch a game from a distance.

Rainbow—Three or four cards of different suits in a flop.

Rake—House percentage. *Also called* Axe, Juice, Snatch, Vig, Vigorish.

Ram and jam—Bet and raise aggressively and often.

Rangdoodles—A temporary increase in bid limit after a certain big hand comes up (like aces full, or better). The next hand doubles the limit. If you've got a game with rangdoodles, set up your opponent to have the big hand, then win the rangdoodles hand yourself. Some people will go double and triple rangdoodles, which is a big payday, but after triple rangdoodles, people will get very suspicious. *See also* Wangdoodle.

Raquel Welch—3–8 as hole cards. It's her bust size (a little flat for my taste).

Rathole—To move chips off the table during play, either secretly or in the open.

Razz—Seven Card Stud lowball.

Readers—Marked cards. *Also called* Papers.

Reamed—What everyone who plays against you will be by the end of the night.

Rembrandt—A draw poker variation where all face cards are wild.

Ribbon clerk—A player who won't play fast or for higher stakes. You don't want them cramping your action, so try to get rid of them.

Ring in—To swap decks in play without being noticed; to change one deck for a cold (stacked) deck.

River—Fifth street. The fifth community card in Hold 'Em; the first three are the flop, followed by the turn, followed by the river.

Rocket—Ace. Two aces in the hole are called "pocket rockets."

Roof—The price of 4 to 1.

Round the World—Similar to Cincinnati, except four cards are in the hole and four cards are the widow.

Rounder—Someone who plays cards for a living, making the rounds.

Royalties—In some games, a fee paid for "premium hands," like aces full or better. Everyone gives a set number of chips to the holder of the hand as a reward. You don't want to take royalties too often, or people notice.

Rumble—To bust a cheat in the middle of a move. Burn.

Runner-runner—A hand made on the last two cards. A runner-runner straight would be hole cards of 2–3 and a flop of

Q–4–10–5–6. Good for getting bets up; people see those as bad beats more than anything else.

Rush—To win several hands in a row; a streak. Sometimes, foolishly attributed to luck.

Saddle—To bend the deck in such a way that the cards will be cut one card above the bend.

Salt away—Remove chips from the table without being noticed. *See* Rathole.

Salty—Having bad luck.

Sandwich—To raise before and after a bettor stuck in the middle. *See* Whipsaw.

Sawbuck—Ten dollars.

Sax—The 6 card.

Scared money—Money that the player is afraid to lose because he can't afford to lose it (and almost certainly will).

Scoop the kitty—Win all the money from all the players at the table. Don't do this too often unless you're burning the game; it'll raise a lot of eyebrows.

Scootermockins—Dollars. Probably German.

Scooting—To scoot is to pass chips from one player to another. Players are not allowed to pass chips in table stakes games, but in friendly home games people don't usually object. If you're in a feelout game, you're going to lose some money anyway, so you can save your poke by ratholing and scooting with a "friend" at the table. They scoot to you, you play with their money, repay them at a later date, and build up trust.

Scourge of Scotland—The 9 of diamonds. They say every ninth king of Scotland was a tyrant, and the diamond is a Scottish symbol.

Screen-out—Distraction used when you're going to make a move. It can be something planned, like pointing out a big play on the

TV, or unplanned, like taking advantage of an accidently spilled drink. *Also called* Shade.

Screwy Louie—A variation on Seven Card Stud where cards are passed several times between players.

Seconds—To deal seconds is to deal while leaving the top card on top of the deck (always dealing the second card).

Set—Three of a kind.

Seven Card Flip—Stud with the first four cards dealt facedown. Each player can flip up any two of their four cards.

Seven Card Pete—(1) Seven Card Stud with all 7s wild. (2) Seven Card Stud with the low card in the hand wild. (3) Seven Card Stud with the low hole card and all cards like it wild. (4) Seven Card Stud with the last hole card dealt and all that are like it as wild.

Seven-Toed Pete—Seven Card Stud.

Shade—*See* Screen-out.

Sharp—Expert player, or a thief. Also called "Shark."

Shaved—(1) Cards that have been trimmed. *Also called* Strippers. (2) To be barely beaten on a hand (like a pair of aces with a jack kicker beating out a pair of aces with a ten kicker).

Shiner—A reflective object used to glimpse the cards during the deal; it can be a mirror, a lighter, or anything shiny.

Shirley—A wimpy, scared player.

Short call—In table stakes, to call part of a bet with all the money you have on the table.

Short money—Less than the normal buy-in for a game.

Sickle—Having A through 4, plus another higher card; a ten-sickle is 10–4–3–2–A.

Side bet—Any bet made between two players; can include low spade, backlines, colors, etc. Side bets are a great way to make some extra scratch during a slow game.

Siegfried and Roy—Q–Q as hole cards.

Sign—Signals between partners about what they're holding. *Also called* Office, Tip the Duke.

Simoleon—One dollar.

Singed—Very close to being burned on a move: Someone noticed something wrong but didn't figure out what happened.

Single-o—A cheater who works alone. It's the only way to go. You want to focus your career on single-o poker.

Six tits—Three queens.

Sizz—Winning several hands in a row is called "putting on a sizz." Don't do this. Win some hands, dump some hands. You win the big ones, they win the small ones.

Skeet—A nonstandard hand; a pelter or kilter.

Skin—(1) To cheat someone. (2) A one-dollar bill.

Skin game—A game with two or more cheats acting as partners. You play in a skin game, you make 50 percent less, unless you've got a fast car.

Skinner—Someone who takes cards out of the game. *See* Hold-out.

Skip straight—A nonstandard hand consisting of every other card in a straight: 2–4–6–8–10, etc. *Also called* a Dutch straight.

Slammer—A long, flat stick covered with a sticky substance that's jammed into a drop box to pull out the rake.

Slug (or slug the deck)—To insert a prearranged stack of cards into the deck to be shuffled into position.

Snatch—The amount taken from each pot in some home games to cover "costs." *Also called* Rake.

Snowmen—8–8 as hole cards.

Southern Cross—A variation of Cincinnati with nine widow cards laid out in a cross.

Spit—A community card.

Spit in the Ocean—A variation of widow poker where the widow card and all cards matching it are wild.

Splash the pot—To toss your chips into the pot, which makes it difficult to tell how much you put in. It's bad form and arouses suspicion, but it works, too.

Spur—To mark cards with your fingernails.

Square—An honest game; not any game that you'll be playing in.

Squeeze—To whipsaw or sandwich another player.

Stack—A packet of cards (or a full deck) prearranged in a certain order.

Stakes—How much you'll be playing for. Usually cash. Bigger stakes are better.

Stand pat—To play a hand without drawing.

Stash—A hidden bankroll; poke.

Steal blinds—To try and win the blinds by representing a good hand; usually done in late position. This does not (necessarily) involve cheating.

Steam—On tilt.

Stenographer—Queen.

Step—A break in the cards, usually for unmaking a cut to put a stack back on top of the deck.

Streak—A run of good cards.

String bets—This is a way of breaking your betting into two parts: You put out the amount of a call while you watch the reaction of the players, and if it looks like you'll get good action, you can then go back and continue the bet. Sometimes this is against the rules, but you can get away with it by calling it a simple misunderstanding.

Strippers—Cards that have been shaved down a fraction of an inch; this lets you pull out nonstripped cards from the deck. This is very dirty work that's hard to explain away, and you're better off learning how to get the cards you need by practicing other techniques.

Stub—The undealt part of the deck. Also called the "talon" or "stock."

Suck out—To get very lucky on the turn or the river for an unlikely save to your hand. Good players expect suck outs, and if you suck out, they'll keep coming at you because they'll know you're lucky. Bad players get frustrated when someone sucks out on the river, and they'll stop playing.

Sweater—A kibitzer.

Table stakes—The rule that a player may only bet money that is on the table at the beginning of a hand; you're also not supposed to remove money from the table during a hand. There are lots of things you're not supposed to do, but you will.

Table talk—Discussing a hand (whether you're in it or out of it) before the hand is over. This is considered rude, but can also be considered cheating—for example, if you were to claim to have folded cards that you didn't have.

Take a bath—To lose a lot of money in one session.

Taking the price—If you get someone to bet on an underdog that you've given odds to, they are taking the price. You want to get your "friends" to take the price on side bets as often as you can.

Talking chips—Someone who has "talking chips" is winning. Your chips won't shut the fuck up.

Tap—"I'm going to tap you" means that you're going to bet all the chips your opponent has, assuming he has fewer than you. When he loses, he's "tapped out," or in "tap city."

Tattooed—Built up a big gambling loss.

Telegraph—To signal between partners; also to give away, as in a tell.

Telephone—A variant of widow poker. Each player gets five facedown cards. Five widow cards. The lowest-value card in a player's hand is wild. Betting happens after players get cards, then after each widow is turned up. Each player makes the best five-card hand from widow and hole cards. Similar to Cincinnati.

Tell—An action that gives away the strength of your hand; this could be subconscious (drumming fingers, playing with a ring) or inadvertent (constantly checking hole cards to see if a hand was made). Mike Caro has "the" book of tells, which any ambitious amateur has read. You can take advantage of this by using "fake tells" to make your opponents think your hand is weak when it's really strong.

Tender hand—A weak favorite, susceptible to being beaten. A midpair preflop, for example. These are good hands to win with, because a tender hand sometimes becomes a powerhouse, if you're "lucky."

Tennessee—A home-game draw variation where bets are made after each card is dealt.

Ten Ten—Five Card Stud with two twists, played hi-lo with ten as the qualifier for low and a pair of tens as the qualifier for high.

Terce—Three cards to a straight flush. If you have A–K–Q of the same suit, that's called "Terce Major."

Test-tube baby—Someone who learned to play cards on a computer and is new to live games.

Texas Tech (Double-Barreled Shotgun)—A type of poker game that's a cross between draw and stud.

"There is work down"—If someone says this to you, they're another card cheat, and they're telling you that there are marked cards in play. Any cheat who announces this should be shot. Get out of his way, and don't partner up with him.

Three Thirty-Three—A game that's a cross between blackjack and hi-lo poker. The object is to get closest to three or thirty-three, with aces and face cards valued as in blackjack. Each player gets one facedown card and can then take as many faceup cards as wanted, with a bet between each round. After all players are done taking cards, they declare (hi, lo, or both). A-A-A is the best hand because it's both 3 and 33, but it's not unbeatable (if someone else has 33, it's a tie for hi and the hi-lo player loses). Other variations are two twenty-two and seven twenty-seven.

Tickle—To raise.

Tiger—A nonstandard hand sometimes counted in home games: five cards between 3 and 9 with no pair, straight, or flush.

Tight—A conservative style of play with fewer (and stronger) hands played. "To tighten up" means "to play tighter."

Tilt—Playing wildly and stupidly. Players often go on tilt due to frustration at losing a hand they should have won; they get impatient and make dumb plays. This is a good opportunity for you, because they start throwing around chips.

Timber—Discarded cards; deadwood. No one cares about these cards except you.

Time—Occasionally a home game will collect time (or have the players "pay time"); card rooms do this instead of a rake; every half hour or hour, every player in the game pays for their seat. In home games, this money often (supposedly) goes for snacks.

Tip the Duke—*See* Sign, Office.

Toad in the Hole—A poker variant of Spit in the Ocean. *Also called* Pig in the Poke.

Toilet flush—A missed flush or four-card flush.

Toke—A tip; "token" of appreciation. *Also called* Zuke.

Token—A chip.

Tom (Tommer)—Slang for bad, as in "a Tom game"; the opposite is "George."

Tool—Any kind of mechanical cheating device, such as a hold-out machine. *Also called* Work.

Top and bottoms—Two pair, aces and deuces.

Topped out—To be beaten by the same hand, only a little bit better. Also called "edged out," "shaved."

Top stock—A prearranged packet of cards on the top of the deck, for use in cheating. If you put your top stock on the bottom and deal from the basement, it's called "bottom stock." If you couldn't figure that out, don't play poker.

Touching cards—These are cards in sequence, like 5–6.

Tough money—Money needed to pay living expenses that can't (shouldn't) be used for gambling. Guess what? People use tough money all the time. It will be yours.

Trade—To receive a twist in home games.

Trey—A 3 card.

Trick—A poor player.

Trims—Skinnies; strippers; pullers; any deck that's been shaved to allow cards to be easily pulled out when reversed.

Trips—Three of a kind.

Trombones—7–6 as hole cards (seventy-six trombones in the big parade).

Tulsa—*See* Omaha.

Tupper—Two pair. Also called "Tupperware."

Turn—The fourth of the community cards after the (three-card) flop; it's followed by the river. *Also called* Fourth street.

Turn down—Fold.

Twiggy—2–9 as hole cards. Comes from the model's measurements. (I'd rather play cards than play with tits that size.)

Twist—In home games, sometimes players can buy a replacement card for one of their up or down cards by putting a preagreed amount in the pot. *See* Optional card. Also called "Substitution," "Discard," "Replacement."

Two bits—Twenty-five dollars.

Two Limit Granny Herschel—A version of Cincinnati for four, six, or eight players; half the players make single bets in a round, the other half make double bets. The winner takes the full pot. *Also called* Granny Herschel.

Two of Three—A variation on Seven Card Stud where you need two out of three of the following to win: high spade, low spade, best hand. Holding ace and 2 of spades guarantees a win.

Two Twenty-Two—A home-game variant of stud where deuces are wild.

Uncle Doc—Five Card Stud with a single widow where all like it are wild.

Undercut—A mechanic's move to get a stack from the bottom of the deck to the top for dealing.

Underdog—Someone who is not statistically favored to win a hand; in other words, everyone you play against.

Under pair—A pair in the hole lower in value than anything on the board; if you have 5–5 and the board shows K–J–8, you have the under pair. These types of hands are good to cheat with, especially if you get a "miracle" on the river, like a third 5. People will think you're a poor player who got lucky, rather than a cheater, and they'll be ready to throw more money at you to win.

Undress—In draw, the call by the dealer for everyone to declare how many cards they want.

Union Oil—7–6 in the hole.

Unit—(1) $1,000. (2) The betting limit of a game.

Up jumped the devil—A phrase some players will say when they get the draw they wanted to make their hand.

Up scope (up the slope, or up the slope went the antelope)—For some reason, some players say this when they raise.

Upstairs—Raise.

V8 Ford Special—Thirteen Card Stud; five cards to each player and eight community cards laid out in a V; one side of the V plays for high, the other side plays for low.

Valet—Jack.

Vig—House percentage taken each hand. *Also Called* Vigorish, Juice, Rake, Axe.

Vigorish—A house percentage. *Also called* Vig, Rake, Axe, Juice.

Village People—Four queens.

Wages—The minimum that you should make per game. Depends on the stakes you play.

Waiter—A person who checks.

Walk—A hand won with only one bet, to which everyone folds. Also, if the big blind wins after everyone folds.

Walk over—Cheat.

Wangdoodle—A hand in which the stakes are temporarily increased, usually after a round in which a premium hand was shown. *See* Rangdoodles.

Wash—To spread the cards on the table and mix them around facedown in big circular movements. It's done to get rid of any steps or stacks, but allows for very easy tracking of specific cards.

Waved cards—Cards that have had a crimp put in the corner.

Weary Willie—Version of poker similar to Cincinnati, but cards in any hand that match widow cards are eliminated from play. *Also called* Elimination.

Weinberg—10–3 as hole cards.

Wheel—The lowest possible straight A–2–3–4–5. Also, the best hand in lowball.

Whipsaw—When two players are in a battle, raising and reraising each other, with a third player (or several players) caught in the middle. This happens both honestly and when two players are in collusion to get the most money out of the guy in the middle; he may get muscled out by the other players. *See* Sandwich, Squeeze. Also called "getting caught in the crossfire."

White blackbird—A completely unlikely hand, such as being dealt a royal straight flush or seeing three aces on a flop.

Whiteskin—A nonpicture card; any card valued 10 or less.

Wide open—On tilt.

Widow—Community cards dealt to the center of the table, part of a number of stud home games like Cincinnati. *Also called* The spit.

Wild—A card that can take on the value of any desired card.

Wild Annie—A poker variation with several betting rounds, a combination of draw and stud.

Wired—A pair in the hole is called a wired pair.

Wooden hand—A hand that's drawing dead; it can't win.

Woolworth—10–5 as hole cards. (Woolworth's was a five-and-dime.)

Work—Cards that have been fixed for cheating. *Also called* Marked cards, Papers.

Work is down—This means that a fixed deck is in play on the table. *See* "There is work down."

Wurlitzer—8–8 as starting cards. (Wurlitzer is a brand of piano, pianos have eighty-eight keys.)

X—Ten dollars. Roman numeral for ten.

Yard—$100.

Yeast—"Give it some yeast" means to raise the pot. This kind of "clever" bullshit will make you want to punch the guy who says it in the nose, but you shouldn't do that. People who say things like this will lose a lot of money to you.

Z-game—The smallest, cheapest game around. *Opposite of* the A-game.

Zuke—A tip. *See also* Toke.

APPENDIX A:
RANK OF WINNING HANDS AND ODDS CHART

Hand	Type	Example	Number of possible hands	Chance of being dealt five cards to make the hand	Odds if you cheat
Five Aces (with Joker)	Freak	A A A A B	1	1 in 2,869,685	1 in 1
Royal Straight Flush	Normal	AS KS QS JS TS	4	1 in 649,740	1 in 1
Five of a Kind (with Joker)	Freak	9 9 9 9 B	13	1 in 220,745	1 in 1
Skeet Flush	Freak	2H 3H 4H 5H 8H	24	1 in 108,290	1 in 1
Straight Flush	Normal	6D 7D 8D 9D TD	40	1 in 64,974	1 in 1
Four Aces	Normal	AAAAX	48	1 in 54,145	1 in 1
Mad Dog (with Joker)	Freak	KS 9S JS 5S X	49	1 in 52,470	1 in 1
Blaze Full	Freak	J J Q Q Q	144	1 in 18,048	1 in 1

Hand	Type	Example	Number of possible hands	Chance of being dealt five cards to make the hand	Odds if you cheat
Big Bobtail	Freak	8C 9C JC QC X	144	1 in 18,048	1 in 1
Four of a Kind	Normal	7 7 7 7 X	624	1 in 4,165	1 in 1
Five of a Kind (with wild cards)	Freak	6 6 6 W W	672	1 in 3,867	1 in 1
Blaze	Freak	P P P P P	792	1 in 3,281	1 in 1
Round the Corner Straight	Freak	J Q K A 2	3,060	1 in 849	1 in 1
Little Bobtail	Freak	4H 5H 6H X X	3,120	1 in 833	1 in 1
Full House	Normal	3 3 8 8 8	3,744	1 in 694	1 in 1
Little Tiger (Little Cat)	Freak	3 X X X 7	4,096	1 in 694	1 in 1
Little Dog	Freak	2 X X X 7	4,096	1 in 634	1 in 1
Five and Dime	Freak	5 X X X10	4,096	1 in 634	1 in 1

H = Hearts · S = Spades · C = Clubs · D = Diamonds · A = Ace ·
K = King · Q = Queen · J = Jack · T = 10 · X = Indifferent card ·
B = Bug (Joker) · P = Any picture card · W = Wild card

Hand	Type	Example	Number of possible hands	Chance of being dealt five cards to make the hand	Odds if you cheat
Big Tiger (Big Cat)	Freak	8 X X X K	4,096	1 in 634	1 in 1
Big Dog	Freak	9 X X X A	4,096	1 in 634	1 in 1
Flush	Normal	D D D D D	5,108	1 in 509	1 in 1
Skeet (Pelter, Bracket)	Freak	2 X 5 X 9	6,144	1 in 423	1 in 1
Skip Straight (Dutch Straight), Kilter	Freak	5 7 9 J K	8,120	1 in 320	1 in 1
Straight	Normal	4 5 6 7 8	10,200	1 in 255	1 in 1
Four Flush with a Pair	Freak	C C C 5C 5	34,320	1 in 76	1 in 1
Three of a Kind	Normal	X X T T T	54,912	1 in 47	1 in 1
Flash (with Joker)	Freak	C H S D B	68,326	1 in 42	1 in 1
Four Flush	Freak	X D D D D	111,540	1 in 23	1 in 1

Hand	Type	Example	Number of possible hands	Chance of being dealt five cards to make the hand	Odds if you cheat
Two Pair	Normal	X 7 7 Q Q	123,552	1 in 21	1 in 1
Pair	Normal	X X X 9 9	1,098,240	1 in 2 3/8	1 in 1
No Pair	Normal	X X X X X	1,302,540	1 in 2	1 in 1

H = Hearts · S = Spades · C = Clubs · D = Diamonds · A = Ace ·
K = King · Q = Queen · J = Jack · T = 10 · X = Indifferent card ·
B = Bug (Joker) · P = Any picture card · W = Wild card

APPENDIX B:
TEN WAYS TO MAKE YOUR HOME POKER GAME CHEAT PROOF

1) Always use standard playing cards with a white border.

Bicycle, Tally-Ho, Kem, or similar brands are good choices. You want a quality card with a white border. The white border makes it more difficult for the cheater to deal seconds.

2) Regularly swap decks in play.

Any player should be able to call for a deck switch at the start of a new hand, and that should be explained to all players. You should always have two decks at the card table, each with a different color back.

3) All shuffling should be done in full view of all the players.

There is never any reason for a deck to be shuffled in someone's lap. With several eyes on the shuffling process, it will be harder for a cheat to manipulate the cards.

4) Keep all money in a small lockbox away from the table.

This will avoid confusion when players buy in or cash out, and the money won't get mixed in with the chips.

5) Only play for big money with people you like or who have good references that you trust.

When games become about the money and not about friendship, there is a much greater temptation for people to cheat. Be a good judge of character, and don't play with people you don't trust. Trust your gut!

6) If extra cards are found on or around a player that you suspect might have been cheating, it's everyone's responsibility to confront that person, not just the host's.

Never jump to conclusions, but calmly try to find out what really happened. Don't encourage violence, but don't be afraid to stop inviting a player back if you have good and sufficient reason to suspect he's cheating. Make sure you're only playing with people you trust.

7) The host of a game is not beyond reproach.

Just because someone is hosting the game doesn't mean that they can't be cheating. What if they set up the game for that purpose? The host of a game has the cards, the chips, and knows the room. If you think someone is cheating, don't rule out the host.

8) Keep drinks and all other items on the table. You don't want hands to disappear from view.

Use cup holders if you're worried about spills and big ashtrays if you're worried about cigarette or cigar burns. You don't want players constantly reaching for drinks and lighters in places where no one can see what they're doing.

9) Play only with chips—no cash on the table.

Cash games encourage temptation. Buying chips allows you to keep track of how much everyone has put in and taken out. In the event that the play of the game has been fouled up, you can at least give everyone back what they started with. Cash games are harder to keep track of.

10) Be aware of pairs of players who talk to each other a lot.

Two players who are constantly chatting (and winning) might be working together. Watch for signals or unusual phrases that are repeated. If two players seem to be working together, you can suggest that people reduce their table talking. You can periodically ask people to switch seats.

INDEX